Naval Battles of the Napoleonic Wars

Naval Battles of the Napoleonic Wars

Cape St. Vincent, the Nile, Cadiz,
Copenhagen, Trafalgar & Others

W. H. Fitchett

LEONAUR

Naval Battles of the Napoleonic Wars: Cape St. Vincent, the Nile,
Cadiz, Copenhagen, Trafalgar & Others
by W. H. Fitchett

Published by Leonaur Ltd

ISBN: 978-1-84677-314-3 (hardcover)
ISBN: 978-1-84677-313-6 (softcover)

http://www.leonaur.com

Publisher's Note

The opinions expressed in this book are those of the author
and are not necessarily those of the publisher.

Contents

Publisher's Note

There has long been a fascination with the exploits of the Royal Navy in the closing years of the eighteenth century and the early years of the nineteenth century. This is a reflection of the fact that Britain had been a great sea power for several centuries and was the pre-eminent naval power of the time. During these momentous years, focused around the brilliance of Horatio Nelson, it can be truly said that Britannia ruled the waves. The names of famous naval commanders of the day, and their equally famous ships are too numerous to list here, as are their decisive battles again the Spanish and Revolutionary France, but their exploits fired the spirit of the nation.

This vital period of British naval history has always captured the imagination and the classic Hornblower novels of C. S. Forrester and, more recently, the novels of Patrick O'Brien, have thousands of devoted readers across the world. However, this book is not a work of fiction but relates instead the true events, horrendous battles and courageous deeds alike, that helped forge an empire and inspired the writers of naval fiction. None of the accounts herein will disappoint, for they reveal the individual acts of courage and daring that are as enthralling as those of any fictional hero.

The Leonaur Editors

CHAPTER 1

The Fight off Cape St. Vincent

On the night of February 13, 1797, an English fleet of fifteen ships of the line, in close order and in readiness for instant battle, was under easy sail off Cape St. Vincent. It was a moonless night, black with haze, and the great ships moved in silence like gigantic spectres over the sea. Every now and again there came floating from the south-east the dull sound of a far-off gun. It was the grand fleet of Spain, consisting of twenty-seven ships of line, under Admiral Don Josef de Cordova; one great ship calling to another through the night, little dreaming that the sound of their guns was so keenly noted by the eager but silent fleet of their enemies to leeward. The morning of the 14th—a day famous in the naval history of the empire—broke dim and hazy; grey sea, grey fog, grey dawn, making all things strangely obscure. At half-past six, however, the keen-sighted British outlooks caught a glimpse of the huge straggling line of Spaniards, stretching apparently through miles of sea haze. "They are thumpers!" as the signal lieutenant of the *Barfleur* reported with emphasis to his captain; "they loom like Beachy Head in a fog!" The Spanish fleet was, indeed, the mightiest ever sent from Spanish ports since "that great fleet invincible" of 1588 carried into the English waters—but not out of them!—"*The richest spoils of Mexico, the stoutest hearts of Spain.*"

The Admiral's flag was borne by the *Santissima Trinidad*, a floating mountain, the largest ship at that time on the sea, and carrying on her four decks 130 guns. Next came six three-deckers carrying 112 guns each, two ships of the line of 80 guns each, and seventeen carrying 74 guns, with no less than twelve 34-gun frigates to act as a flying cordon of skirmishers. Spain had joined France against England on September 12, 1796, and Don Cordova, at the head of this immense fleet, had sailed from Cadiz to execute a daring and splendid strategy. He was to pick up the Toulon fleet, brush away the English squadron blockading Brest, add the great French fleet lying imprisoned there to his forces, and enter the British Channel with above a hundred sail of the line under his flag, and sweep in triumph to the mouth of the Thames! If the plan succeeded, Portugal would fall, a descent was to be made on Ireland; the British flag, it was reckoned, would be swept from the seas.

Sir John Jervis was lying in the track of the Spaniards to defeat this ingenious plan. Five ships of the line had been withdrawn from the squadron blockading Brest to strengthen him; still he had only fifteen ships against the twenty-seven huge Spaniards in front of him; whilst, if the French Toulon fleet behind him broke out, he ran the risk of being crushed, so to speak, betwixt the upper and the nether millstone. Never, perhaps, was the naval supremacy of England challenged so boldly and with such a prospect of success as at this moment. The northern powers had coalesced under Russia, and only a few weeks later the English guns were thundering over the roofs of Copenhagen, while the united flags of France and Spain were preparing to sweep through the narrow seas. The "splendid isolation" of to-day is no novelty. In 1796, as it threatened to be in

Spanish Windward
Division

11h. A.M.

Spanish Lee Division

British

THE BATTLE OFF CAPE ST. VINCENT.
Cutting the Spanish Line.

1896, Great Britain stood singly against a world in arms, and it is scarcely too much to say that her fate hung on the fortunes of the fleet that, in the grey dawn of St. Valentine's Day, a hundred years ago, was searching the skyline for the topmasts of Don Cordova's huge three-deckers.

Fifteen to twenty-seven is enormous odds, but, on the testimony of Nelson himself, a better fleet never carried the fortunes of a great country than that under Sir John Jervis. The mere names of the ships or of their commanders awaken more sonorous echoes than the famous catalogue of the ships in the "Iliad." Trowbridge, in the *Culloden*, led the van; the line was formed of such ships as the *Victory*, the flagship, the *Barfleur*, the *Blenheim*, the *Captain*, with Nelson as commodore, the *Excellent*, under Collingwood, the *Colossus*, under Murray, the *Orion*, under Sir James Saumarez, &c. Finer sailors and more daring leaders never bore down upon an enemy's fleet. The picture offered by the two fleets in the cold haze of that fateful morning, as a matter of fact, reflected the difference in their fighting and sea-going qualities. The Spanish fleet, a line of monsters, straggled, formless and shapeless, over miles of sea space, distracted with signals, fluttering with many-coloured flags. The English fleet, grim and silent, bore down upon the enemy in two compact and firm-drawn columns, ship following ship so closely and so exactly that bowsprit and stern almost touched, while an air-line drawn from the foremast of the leading ship to the mizzenmast of the last ship in each column would have touched almost every mast betwixt. Stately, measured, threatening, in perfect fighting order, the compact line of the British bore down on the Spaniards.

Nothing is more striking in the battle of St. Vincent than the swift and resolute fashion in which Sir John Jervis leaped, so to speak, at his enemy's throat, with the silent but deadly leap of a bulldog. As the fog lifted, about nine o'clock, with the suddenness and dramatic effect of the lifting of a curtain in a great theatre, it revealed to the British admiral a great opportunity. The weather division of the Spanish fleet, twenty-one gigantic ships, resembled nothing so much as a confused and swaying forest of masts; the leeward division—six ships in a cluster, almost as confused—was parted by an interval of nearly three miles from the main body of the fleet, and into that fatal gap, as with the swift and deadly thrust of a rapier, Jervis drove his fleet in one unswerving line, the two columns melting into one, ship following hard on ship. The Spaniards strove furiously to close their line, the twenty-one huge ships bearing down from the windward, the smaller squadron clawing desperately up from the leeward. But the British fleet—a long line of gliding pyramids of sails, leaning over to the pressure of the wind, with "the meteor flag" flying from the peak of each vessel, and the curving lines of guns awaiting grim and silent beneath—was too swift. As it swept through the gap, the Spanish vice-admiral, in the *Principe de Asturias*, a great three-decker of 112 guns, tried the daring feat of breaking through the British line to join the severed squadron. He struck the English fleet almost exactly at the flagship, the *Victory*. The *Victory* was thrown into stays to meet her, the Spaniard swung round in response, and, exactly as her quarter was exposed to the broadside of the *Victory*, the thunder of a tremendous broadside rolled from that ship. The unfortunate Spaniard was smitten as with a tempest of iron, and the next moment, with sails torn, topmasts hanging to leeward, ropes hanging loose in every direction, and her decks splashed red with the blood of her slaughtered crew, she broke off to windward. The iron line of the British was unpierceable! The leading three-decker of the Spanish lee division in like manner bore up, as though to break through the British line to join her admiral; but the grim succession of three-deckers, following swift on each other like the links of a moving iron chain, was too disquieting a prospect to be faced. It was not in Spanish seamanship, or, for the matter of that, in Spanish flesh and blood, to beat up in the teeth of such threatening lines of iron lips. The Spanish ships swung sullenly back to leeward, and the fleet of Don Cordova was cloven in twain, as though by the stroke of some gigantic sword-blade.

As soon as Sir John Jervis saw the steady line of his fleet drawn fair across the gap in the Spanish line, he flung his leading ships up to windward on the mass of the Spanish fleet, by this time beating up to windward. The *Culloden* led, thrust itself betwixt the hindmost Spanish three-deckers, and broke into flame and thunder on either side. Six minutes after her came the *Blenheim*; then, in quick succession, the *Prince George*, the *Orion*, the *Colossus*. It was a crash of swaying masts and bellying sails, while below rose the shouting of the crews, and, like the thrusts of fiery swords, the flames shot out from the sides of the great three-deckers against each other, and over all rolled the thunder and the smoke of a Titanic sea-fight. Nothing more murderous than close fighting betwixt the huge wooden ships of those days can well be imagined. The *Victory*, the largest British ship present in the action, was only 186 feet long and 52 feet broad; yet in that little area 1000 men fought, 100 great guns thundered. A Spanish ship like the *San Josef* was 194 feet in length and 54 feet in breadth; but in that area 112 guns were mounted, while the three decks were thronged with some 1300 men. When floating batteries like these swept each other with the flame of swiftly repeated broadsides at a distance of a few score yards, the destruction may be better imagined than described. The Spanish had an advantage in the number of guns and men, but the British established an instant mastery by their silent discipline, their perfect seamanship, and the speed with which their guns were worked. They fired at least three broadsides to every two the Spaniards discharged, and their fire had a deadly precision compared with which that of the Spaniards was mere distracted spluttering.

Meanwhile the dramatic crisis of the battle came swiftly on. The Spanish admiral was resolute to join the severed fragments of his fleet. The *Culloden*, the *Blenheim*, the *Prince George*, and the *Orion* were thundering amongst his rearmost ships, and as the British line swept up, each ship tacked as it crossed the gap in the Spanish line, bore up to windward and added the thunder of its guns to the storm of battle raging amongst the hindmost Spaniards. But naturally the section of the British line that had not yet passed the gap shortened with every minute, and the leading Spanish ships at last saw the sea to their leeward clear of the enemy, and the track open to their own lee squadron. Instantly they swung round to leeward, the great four-decker, the flagship, with a company of sister giants, the *San Josef* and the *Salvador del Mundo*, of 112 guns each, the *San Nicolas*, and three other great ships of 80 guns. It was a bold and clever stroke. This great squadron, with the breeze behind it, had but to sweep past the rear of the British line, join the lee squadron, and bear up, and the Spanish fleet in one unbroken mass would confront the enemy. The rear of the British line was held by Collingwood in the *Excellent*; next to him came the

Diadem; the third ship was the *Captain*, under Nelson. We may imagine how Nelson's solitary eye was fixed on the great Spanish three-deckers that formed the Spanish van as they suddenly swung round and came sweeping down to cross his stern. Not Napoleon himself had a vision more swift and keen for the changing physiognomy of a great battle than Nelson, and he met the Spanish admiral with a counter-stroke as brilliant and daring as can be found in the whole history of naval warfare. The British fleet saw the *Captain* suddenly swing out of line to leeward—in the direction from the Spanish line, that is—but with swift curve the *Captain* doubled back, shot between the two English ships that formed the rear of the line, and bore up straight in the path of the Spanish flagship, with its four decks, and the huge battleships on either side of it.

The *Captain*, it should be remembered, was the smallest 74 in the British fleet, and as the great Spanish ships closed round her and broke into flame it seemed as if each one of them was big enough to hoist the *Captain* on board like a jolly-boat. Nelson's act was like that of a single stockman who undertakes to "head off" a drove of angry bulls as they break away from the herd; but the "bulls" in this case were a group of the mightiest battleships then afloat. Nelson's sudden movement was a breach of orders; it left a gap in the British line; to dash unsupported into the Spanish van seemed mere madness, and the spectacle, as the Captain opened fire on the huge *Santissima Trinidad*, was simply amazing. Nelson was in action at once with the flagship of 130 guns, two ships of 112 guns, one of 80 guns, and two of 74 guns! To the spectators who watched the sight the sides of the *Captain* seemed to throb with quick-following pulses of flame as its crew poured their shot into the huge hulks on every side of them. The Spaniards formed a mass so tangled that they could scarcely fire at the little *Captain* without injuring each other; yet the English ship seemed to shrivel beneath even the imperfect fire that did reach her. Her foremast was shot away, her wheel-post shattered, her rigging torn, some of her guns dismantled, and the ship was practically incapable of further service either in the line or in chase. But Nelson had accomplished his purpose: he had stopped the rush of the Spanish van.

At this moment the *Excellent*, under Collingwood, swept into the storm of battle that raged round the *Captain*, and poured three tremendous broadsides into the Spanish three-decker the *Salvador del Mundo* that practically disabled her. "We were not further from her," the domestic but hard-fighting Collingwood wrote to his wife, "than the length of our garden." Then, with a fine feat of seamanship, the *Excellent* passed between the *Captain* and the *San Nicolas*, scourging that unfortunate ship with flame at a distance of ten yards, and then passed on to bestow its favours on the *Santissima Trinidad*—"such a ship," Collingwood afterwards confided to his wife, "as I never saw before!" Collingwood tormented that monster with his fire so vehemently that she actually struck, though possession of her was not taken before the other Spanish ships, coming up, rescued her, and she survived to carry the Spanish flag in the great fight of Trafalgar.

Meanwhile the crippled *Captain*, though actually disabled, had performed one of the most dramatic and brilliant feats in the history of naval warfare. Nelson put his helm to starboard, and ran, or rather drifted, on the quarter-gallery of the *San Nicolas*, and at once boarded that leviathan. Nelson himself crept through the quarter-gallery window in the stern of the Spaniard, and found himself in the officers' cabins. The officers tried to show fight, but there was no denying the boarders who followed Nelson, and with shout and oath, with flash of pistol and ring of steel, the party swept through on to the main deck. But the *San Nicolas* had been boarded also at other points. "The first man who jumped into the enemy's mizzen-chains," says Nelson, "was the first lieutenant of the ship, afterwards Captain Berry." The English sailors dropped from their spritsail yard on to the Spaniard's deck, and by the time Nelson reached the poop of the *San Nicolas* he found his lieutenant in the act of hauling down the Spanish flag. Nelson proceeded to collect the swords of the Spanish officers, when a fire was opened upon them from the stern gallery of the admiral's ship, the *San Josef*, of 112 guns, whose sides were grinding against those of the *San Nicolas*. What could Nelson do? To keep his prize he must assault a still bigger ship. Of course he never hesitated! He flung his boarders up the side of the huge *San Josef*, but he himself had to be assisted to climb the main chains of that vessel, his lieutenant this time dutifully assisting his commodore up instead of indecorously going ahead of him. "At this moment," as Nelson records the incident, "a Spanish officer looked over the quarter-deck rail and said they surrendered. It was not long before I was on the quarter-deck, where the Spanish captain, with a bow, presented me his sword, and said the admiral was dying of his wounds. I asked him, on his honour, if the ship was surrendered. He declared she was; on which I gave him my hand, and desired him to call on his officers and ship's company and tell them of it, which he did; and on the quarterdeck of a Spanish first-rate—extravagant as the story may seem—did I receive the swords of vanquished

Spaniards, which, as I received, I gave to William Fearney, one of my bargemen, who put them with the greatest *sang-froid* under his arm," a circle of "old Agamemnons," with smoke-blackened faces, looking on in grim approval.

This is the story of how a British fleet of fifteen vessels defeated a Spanish fleet of twenty-seven, and captured four of their finest ships. It is the story, too, of how a single English ship, the smallest 74 in the fleet—but made unconquerable by the presence of Nelson—stayed the advance of a whole squadron of Spanish three-deckers, and took two ships, each bigger than itself, by boarding. Was there ever a finer deed wrought under "the meteor flag"! Nelson disobeyed orders by leaving the English line and flinging himself on the van of the Spaniards, but he saved the battle. Calder, Jervis's captain, complained to the admiral that Nelson had "disobeyed orders."

"He certainly did," answered Jervis; "and if ever you commit such a breach of your orders I will forgive you also."

CHAPTER 2

The Recapture of the *Hermione*

The story of how the *Hermione* was lost is one of the scandals and the tragedies of British naval history; the tale of how it was re-won is one of its glories. The *Hermione* was a 32-gun frigate, cruising off Porto Rico, in the West Indies. On the evening of September 21, 1797, the men were on drill, reefing topsails. The captain, Pigot, was a rough and daring sailor, a type of the brutal school of naval officer long extinct. The traditions of the navy were harsh; the despotic power over the lives and fortunes of his crew which the captain of a man-of-war carried in the palm of his hand, when made the servant of a ferocious temper, easily turned a ship into a floating hell. The terrible mutinies which broke out in British fleets two hundred years ago had some justification, at least, in the cruelties, as well as the hardships, to which the sailors of that period were exposed.

Pigot was rough in speech, vehement in temper, cursed with a semi-lunatic delight in cruelty, and he tormented his men to the verge of desperation. On this fatal night, Pigot, standing at the break of his quarter-deck, stormed at the men aloft, and swore with many oaths he would flog the last man off the mizzentop yard; and the men knew how well he would keep his word. The most active sailor, as the men lay out on the yard, naturally takes the earing, and is, of course, the last man off, as well as on, the yard. Pigot's method, that is, would punish not the worst sailors, but the best! The two outermost men on the mizzen-top yard of the *Hermione* that night, determined to escape the threatened flogging. They made a desperate spring to get over their comrades crowding into the ratlines, missed their foothold, fell on the quarter-deck beside their furious captain, and were instantly killed. The captain's epitaph on the unfortunate sailors was, "Throw the lubbers overboard!"

All the next day a sullen gloom lay on the ship. Mutiny was breeding. It began, as night fell, in a childish fashion, by the men throwing double-headed shot about the deck. The noise brought down the first lieutenant to restore order. He was knocked down. In the jostle of fierce tempers, murder awoke; knives gleamed. A sailor, as he bent over the fallen officer, saw the naked undefended throat, and thrust his knife into it. The sight kindled the men's passions to flame. The unfortunate lieutenant was killed with a dozen stabs, and his body thrown overboard. The men had now tasted blood. In the flame of murderous temper suddenly let loose, all the bonds of discipline were in a moment consumed. A wild rush was made for the officers' cabins. The captain tried to break his way out, was wounded, and driven back; the men swept in, and, to quote the realistic official account, "seated in his cabin the captain was stabbed by his own coxswain and three other mutineers, and, forced out of the cabin windows, was heard to speak as he went astern." With mutiny comes anarchy. The men made no distinction between their officers, cruel or gentle; not only the captain, but the three lieutenants, the purser, the surgeon, the lieutenant of marines, the boatswain, the captain's clerk were murdered, and even one of the two midshipmen on board was hunted like a rat through the ship, killed, and thrown overboard. The only officers spared were the master, the gunner, and one midshipman.

Having captured the ship, the mutineers were puzzled how to proceed. Every man-of-war on the station, they knew, would be swiftly on their track. Every British port was sealed to them. They would be pursued by a retribution which would neither loiter nor slumber. On the open sea there was no safety for mutineers. They turned the head of the *Hermione* towards the nearest Spanish port, La Guayra, and, reaching it, surrendered the ship to the Spanish authorities, saying they had turned their officers adrift in the jolly-boat. The Spaniards were not disposed to scrutinise too closely the story. A transaction which put into their hands a fine British frigate was welcomed with rapture. The British admiral in command of the station sent in a flag of truce with the true account of the mutiny, and called upon the Spanish authorities, as a matter of honour, to surrender the *Hermione*, and hand over for punishment the murderers who had carried it off. The appeal, however, was wasted.

The *Hermione*, a handsome ship of 715 tons, when under the British flag, was armed with thirty-two 12-pounders, and had a complement of 220 men. The Spaniards cut new ports in her, increased her broadsides to forty-four guns, and gave her a complement, including a detachment of soldiers and artillerymen, of nearly 400 men. She thus became the most formidable ship carrying the Spanish flag in West Indian waters.

But the *Hermione*, under its new flag, had a very anxious existence. It became a point of honour with every British vessel on the station to look out for the ship which had become the symbol of mutiny, and make a dash at her, no matter what the odds. The brutal murders which attended the mutiny shocked even the forecastle imagination, while the British officers were naturally eager to destroy the ship which represented revolt against discipline. Both fore and aft, too, the fact that what had been a British frigate was now carrying the flag of Spain was resented with a degree of exasperation which assured to the *Hermione*, under its new name and flag, a very warm time if it came under the fire of a British ship. The Spaniards kept the *Hermione* for just two years, but kept her principally in port, as the moment she showed her nose in the open sea some British ship or other, sleeplessly on the watch for her, bore down with disconcerting eagerness.

In September 1799 the *Hermione* was lying in Puerto Cabello, while the *Surprise*, a 28-gun frigate, under Captain Edward Hamilton, was waiting outside, specially detailed by the admiral, Sir Hyde Parker, to attack her the instant she put to sea. The *Surprise* had less than half the complement of the *Hermione*, and not much more than half her weight of metal. But Hamilton was not only willing to fight the *Hermione* in the open sea against such odds; he told the admiral that if he would give him a barge and twenty men he would undertake to carry the *Hermione* with his boats while lying in harbour. Parker pronounced the scheme too desperate to be entertained, and refused Hamilton the additional boat's crew for which he asked. Yet this was the very plan which Hamilton actually carried out without the reinforcement for which he had asked!

Hamilton, to tempt the *Hermione* out, kept carefully out of sight of Puerto Cabello to leeward, yet in such a position that if the *Hermione* left the harbour her topsails must become visible to the look-outs on the mastheads of the *Surprise*; and he kept that post until his provisions failed. Then, as the *Hermione* would not come out to him, he determined to go into the *Hermione*. Hamilton was a silent, much-meditating man, not apt to share his counsels with anybody. In the cells of his brooding and solitary brain he prepared, down to the minutest details, his plan for a dash at the *Hermione*—a ship, it must be remembered, not only more than double his own in strength, but lying moored head and stern in a strongly fortified port, under the fire of batteries mounting nearly 200 guns, and protected, in addition, by several gunboats. In a boat attack, too, Hamilton could carry only part of his crew with him; he must leave enough hands on board his own ship to work her. As a matter of fact, he put in his boats less than 100 men, and with them, in the blackness of night, rowed off to attack a ship that carried 400 men, and was protected by the fire, including her own broadsides, of nearly 300 guns! The odds were indeed so great that the imagination of even British sailors, if allowed to meditate long upon them, might become chilled. Hamilton therefore breathed not a whisper of his plans, even to his officers, till he was ready to put them into execution, and, when he did announce them, carried them out with cool but unfaltering speed.

On the evening of October 24, Hamilton invited all the officers not on actual duty to dine in his cabin. The scene may be easily pictured. The captain at the head of his table, the merry officers on either side, the jest, the laughter, the toasts; nobody there but the silent, meditative captain dreaming of the daring deed to be that night attempted. When dinner was over, and the officers alone, with a gesture Hamilton arrested the attention of the party, and ex-

plained in a few grim sentences his purpose. The little party
of brave men about him listened eagerly and with kindling
eyes. "We'll stand by you, captain," said one. "We'll all follow
you," said another. Hamilton bade his officers follow him
at once to the quarter-deck. A roll of the drum called the
men instantly to quarters, and, when the officers reported
every man at his station, they were all sent aft to where, on
the break of the quarter-deck, the captain waited.

It was night, starless and black, but a couple of lanterns
shed a few broken rays on the massed seamen with their
wondering, upturned faces, and the tall figure of the silent
captain. Hamilton explained in a dozen curt sentences that
they must run into port for supplies; that if they left their
station some more fortunate ship would have the glory of
taking the *Hermione*. "Our only chance, lads," he added, "is
to cut her out to-night!" As that sentence, with a keen ring
on its last word, swept over the attentive sailors, they made
the natural response, a sudden growling cheer. "I lead you
myself," added Hamilton, whereupon came another cheer;
"and here are the orders for the six boats to be employed,
with the names of the officers and men." Instantly the
crews were mustered, while the officers, standing in a cluster round the captain, heard the details of the expedition.
Every seaman was to be dressed in blue, without a patch
of white visible; the password was "Britannia," the answer
"Ireland"—Hamilton himself being an Irishman.

By half-past seven the boats were actually hoisted out
and lowered, the men armed and in their places, and each
little crew instructed as to the exact part it was to play
in the exciting drama. The orders given were curiously
minute. The launch, for example, was to board on the starboard bow, but three of its men, before boarding, were first

to cut the bower cable, for which purpose a little platform was rigged up on the launch's quarter, and sharp axes provided. The jolly-boat was to board on the starboard quarter, cut the stern cable, and send two men aloft to loose the mizzen topsail. The gig, under the command of the doctor, was to board on the larboard bow, and instantly send four men aloft to loose the fore topsail. If the *Hermione* was reached without any alarm being given, only the boarders were to leap on board; the ordinary crews of the boats were to take the frigate in tow. Thus, if Hamilton's plans were carried out, the Spaniards would find themselves suddenly boarded at six different points, their cables cut, their topsails dropped, and their ship being towed out—and all this at the same instant of time. "The rendezvous," said Hamilton to his officers, as the little cluster of boats drew away from the *Surprise*, "is the *Hermione's* quarter-deck!"

Hamilton himself led, standing up in his pinnace, with his night-glass fixed on the doomed ship, and the boats followed with stern almost touching stern, and a rope passed from each boat to the one behind. Can a more impressive picture of human daring be imagined than these six boats pulling silently ever the black waters and through the black night to fling themselves, under the fire of two hundred guns, on a foe four times more numerous than themselves! The boats had stolen to within less than a mile of the *Hermione*, when a Spanish challenge rang out of the darkness before them. Two Spanish gunboats were on guard within the harbour, and they at once opened fire on the chain of boats gliding mysteriously through the gloom. There was no longer any possibility of surprise, and Hamilton instantly threw off the rope that connected him with the next boat and shouted to his men to pull. The men, with a loud "Hurrah!" dashed their oars into the water, and the boats leaped forward towards the *Hermione*. But Hamilton's boats—two of them commanded by midshipmen—could not find themselves so close to a couple of Spanish gunboats without "going" for them. Two of the six boats swung aside and dashed at the gunboats; only three followed Hamilton at the utmost speed towards the *Hermione*.

That ship, meanwhile, was awake. Lights flashed from every port; a clamour of voices broke on the quiet of the night; the sound of the drum rolled along the decks, the men ran to quarters. Hamilton, in the pinnace, dashed past the bows of the *Hermione* to reach his station, but a rope, stretched from the *Hermione* to her anchor-buoy, caught the rudder of the pinnace and stopped her in full course, the coxswain reporting the boat "aground." The pinnace had swung round till her starboard oars touched the bend of the *Hermione*, and Hamilton gave the word to "board." Hamilton himself led, and swung himself up till his feet rested on the anchor hanging from the *Hermione's* cat-head. It was covered with mud, having been weighed that day, and his feet slipping off it, Hamilton hung by the lanyard of the *Hermione's* foreshroud. The crew of the pinnace meanwhile climbing with the agility of cats and the eagerness of boys, had tumbled over their own captain's shoulders as well as the bulwarks of the *Hermione*, and were on that vessel's forecastle, where Hamilton in another moment joined them. Here were sixteen men on board a vessel with a hostile crew four hundred strong.

Hamilton ran to the break of the forecastle and looked down, and to his amazement found the whole crew of the *Hermione* at quarters on the main-deck, with battle-lanterns lit, and firing with the utmost energy at the darkness, in which their excited fancy saw the tall masts of at least a squadron of frigates bearing down to attack them. Hamilton, followed by his fifteen men, ran aft to the agreed rendezvous on the *Hermione's* quarter-deck. The doctor, with his crew, had meantime boarded, and forgetting all about the rendezvous, and obeying only the natural fighting impulse in their own blood, charged upon the Spaniards in the gangway.

Hamilton sent his men down to assist in the fight, waiting alone on the quarter-deck till his other boat boarded. Here four Spaniards rushed suddenly upon him; one struck him over the head with a musket with a force that broke the weapon itself, and knocked him semi-senseless upon the combings of the hatchway. Two British sailors, who saw their commander's peril, rescued him, and, with blood streaming down from his battered head upon his uniform, Hamilton flung himself into the fight at the gangway. At this juncture the black cutter, in command of the first lieutenant, with the *Surprise's* marines on board, dashed up to the side of the *Hermione*, and the men came tumbling over the larboard gangway. They had made previously two unsuccessful attempts to board. They came up first by the steps of the larboard gangway, the lieutenant leading. He was incontinently knocked down, and tumbled all his men with him as he fell back into the boat. They then tried the starboard of the *Hermione*, and were again beaten back, and only succeeded on a third attempt.

Three boats' crews of the British were now together on the deck of the *Hermione*. They did not number fifty men in all, but the marines were instantly formed up and a volley was fired down the after hatchway. Then, following the flash of their muskets, with the captain leading, the whole party leaped down upon the maindeck, driving the Spaniards before them. Some sixty Spaniards took refuge in the cabin, and shouted they surrendered, whereupon they were ordered to throw down their arms, and the doors were locked upon them, turning them into prisoners. On the main-deck and under the fore-castle, however, the fighting was fierce and deadly; but by this time the other boats had come up, and the cables fore and aft were cut, as had been arranged. The men detailed for that task had raced up the Spaniard's rigging, and while the desperate fight raged below, had cast loose the topsails of the *Hermione*. Three of the boats, too, had taken her in tow. She began to move seaward, and that movement, with the sound of the rippling water along the ship's sides, appalled the Spaniards, and persuaded them the ship was lost.

On the quarter-deck the gunner and two men—all three wounded—stood at the wheel, and flung the head of the *Hermione* seaward. They were fiercely attacked, but while one man clung to the wheel and kept control of the ship, the gunner and his mate kept off the Spaniards. Presently the foretopsail filled with the land breeze, the water rippled louder along the sides of the moving vessel, the ship swayed to the wind. The batteries by this time were thundering from the shore, but though they shot away many ropes, they fired with signal ill-success. Only fifty British sailors and marines, it must be remembered, were actually on the deck of the *Hermione*, and amongst the crowd of sullen and exasperated Spaniards below, who had surrendered, but were still furious with the aston-ishment of the attack and the passion of the fight, there arose a shout to "blow up the ship." The British had to fire down through the hatchway upon the swaying crowd to enforce order. By two o'clock the struggle was over, the *Hermione* was beyond the fire of the batteries, and the crews of the boats towing her came on board.

There is no more surprising fight in British history. The mere swiftness with which the adventure was carried out is marvellous. It was past six P.M. when Hamilton disclosed his plan to his officers, the *Hermione* at that moment lying some eight miles distant; by two o'clock the captured ship, with the British flag flying from her peak, was clear of the harbour. Only half a hundred men actually got on board the *Hermione*, but what a resolute, hard-smiting, strong-fisted band they were may be judged by the results. Of the Spaniards, 119 were killed, and 97 wounded, most of them dangerously. Hamilton's 50 men, that is, in those few minutes of fierce fighting, cut down four times their own number! Not one of the British, as it happened, was killed, and only 12 wounded, Captain Hamilton himself receiving no less than five serious wounds. The *Hermione* was restored to her place in the British Navy List, but under a new name—the *Retribution*—and the story of that heroic night attack will be for all time one of the most stirring incidents in the long record of brave deeds performed by British seamen.

CHAPTER 3

The Battle of the Nile

Aboukir Bay resembles nothing so much as a piece bitten out of the Egyptian pancake. A crescent-shaped bay, patchy with shoals, stretching from the Rosetta mouth of the Nile to Aboukir, or, as it is now called, Nelson Island, that island being simply the outer point of a sandbank that projects from the western horn of the bay. Flat shores, grey-blue Mediterranean waters, two horns of land six miles apart, that to the north projecting farthest and forming a low island—this, two hundred years ago, was the scene of what might almost be described as the greatest sea-fight in history.

On the evening of August 1, 1798, thirteen great battleships lay drawn up in a single line parallel with the shore, and as close to it as the sandbanks permitted. The head ship was almost stern on to the shoal which, running out at right angles to the shore, forms Aboukir Island. The nose of each succeeding ship was exactly 160 yards from the stern of the ship before it, and, allowing for one or two gaps, each ship was bound by a great cable to its neighbour. It was a thread of beads, only each "bead" was a battleship, whose decks swarmed with brave men, and from whose sides gaped the iron lips of more than a thousand heavy guns. The line was not exactly straight; it formed a very obtuse angle, the projecting point at the centre being formed by the *Orient*, the biggest warship at that moment afloat, a giant of 120 guns.

Next to her came the *Franklin*, of 80 guns, a vessel which, if not the biggest, was perhaps the finest sample of naval architecture in existence. The line of ships was more than one mile and a half long, and consisted of the gigantic flagship, three ships of the line of 80 guns, and nine of 74 guns. In addition, it had a fringe of gunboats and frigates, while a battery of mortars on the island guarded, as with a sword of fire, the gap betwixt the headmost ship and the island. This great fleet had convoyed Napoleon, with 36,000 troops crowded into 400 transports, from France, had captured Malta on the voyage, and three weeks before had safely landed Napoleon and his soldiers in Egypt. The French admiral, Bruéys, knew that Nelson was coming furiously in his track, and after a consultation with all his captains he had drawn up his ships in the order which we have described, a position he believed to be unassailable. And at three o'clock on the afternoon of August 1, 1798, his look-outs were eagerly watching the white topsails showing above the lee line, the van of Nelson's fleet.

Napoleon had kept the secret of his Egyptian expedition well, and the great Toulon fleet, with its swarm of transports, had vanished round the coast of Corsica and gone off into mere space, as far as a bewildered British Admiralty knew. A fleet of thirteen 74-gun ships and one of 50 guns was placed under Nelson's flag. He was ordered to pursue and destroy the vanished French fleet, and with characteristic energy he set out on one of the most dramatic sea-chases known to history. With the instinct of genius he guessed that Napoleon's destination was Egypt; but while the French fleet coasted Sardinia and went to the west of

Sicily, Nelson ran down the Italian coast to Naples, called there for information, found none, and, carrying all sail, swept through the straits of Messina.

On the night of June 22 the two fleets actually crossed each other's tracks. The French fleet, including the transports, numbered 572 vessels, and their lights, it might be imagined, would have lit up many leagues of sea. Yet, through this forest of hostile masts the English fleet, with keen eyes watching at every masthead, swept and saw nothing. Nelson, for one thing, had no frigates to serve as eyes and ears for him; his fleet in sailor-like fashion formed a compact body, three parallel lines of phantom-like pyramids of canvas sweeping in the darkness across the floor of the sea. Above all a haze filled the night; and it is not too much to say that the drifting grey vapour which hid the French ships from Nelson's lookout men changed the face of history.

Nelson used to explain that his ideal of perfect enjoyment would be to have the chance of "trying Bonaparte on a wind"; and if he had caught sound of bell or gleam of lantern from the great French fleet, and brought it to action in the darkness of that foggy night, can any one doubt what the result would have been? Nelson would have done off the coast of Sicily on June 22, 1798, what Wellington did on June 18, 1815; and in that case there would have been no Marengo or Austerlitz, no retreat from Moscow, no Peninsular war, and no Waterloo. For so much, in distracted human affairs, may a patch of drifting vapour count!

Nelson, in a word, overran his prey. He reached Alexandria to find the coast empty; doubled back to Sicily, zigzagging on his way by Cyprus and Candia; and twelve hours after he had left Alexandria the topsails of the French fleet hove in sight from that port. Napoleon's troops were safely

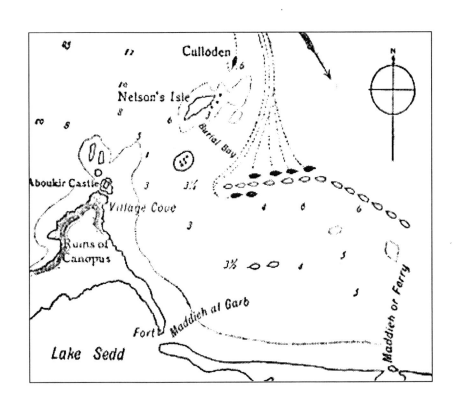

landed, and the French admiral had some four weeks in which to prepare for Nelson's return, and at 3 P.M. on August 1 the gliding topsails of the *Swiftsure* above Aboukir Island showed that the tireless Englishman had, after nearly three months of pursuit, overtaken his enemy.

The French, if frigates be included, counted seventeen ships to fourteen, and ship for ship they had the advantage over the British alike in crew, tonnage, and weight of fire. In size the English ships scarcely averaged 1500 tons, the French ships exceeded 2000 tons. Nelson had only seventy-fours, his heaviest gun being a 32-pounder. The average French 80-gun ship in every detail of fighting strength exceeded an English ninety-eight, and Bruéys had three such ships in his fleet; while his own flagship, the *Orient*, was fully equal to two English seventy-fours. Its weight of ball on the lower deck alone exceeded that from the whole broadside of the *Bellerophon*, the ship that engaged it. The French, in brief, had an advantage in guns of about twenty per cent., and in men of over thirty per cent. Bruéys, moreover, was lying in a carefully chosen position in a dangerous bay, of which his enemies possessed no chart, and the head of his line was protected by a powerful shore battery.

Nothing in this great fight is more dramatic than the swiftness and vehemence of Nelson's attack. He simply leaped upon his enemy at sight. Four of his ships were miles off in the offing, but Nelson did not wait for them. In the long pursuit he had assembled his captains repeatedly in his cabin, and discussed every possible manner of attacking the French fleet. If he found the fleet as he guessed, drawn up in battle-line close in-shore and anchored, his plan was to place one of his ships on the bows, another on the quarter, of each French ship in succession.

It has been debated who actually evolved the idea of rounding the head of the French line and attacking on both faces. One version is that Foley, in the *Goliath*, who led the British line, owed the suggestion to a keen-eyed middy who pointed out that the anchor buoy of the headmost French ship was at such a distance from the ship itself as to prove there was room to pass. But the weight of evidence seems to prove that Nelson himself, as he rounded Aboukir Island, and scanned with fierce and questioning vision Bruéys' formation, with that swiftness of glance in which he almost rivalled Napoleon, saw his chance in the gap between the leading French ship and the shore. "Where a French ship can swing," he held, "an English ship can either sail or anchor." And he determined to double on the French line and attack on both faces at once. He explained his plan to Berry, his captain, who in his delight exclaimed, "If we succeed, what will the world say?" "There is no 'if' in the case," said Nelson; "that we shall succeed is certain; who will live to tell the story is a very different question."

Bruéys had calculated that the English fleet must come down perpendicularly to his centre, and each ship in the process be raked by a line of fire a mile and a half long; but the moment the English ships rounded the island they tacked, hugged the shore, and swept through the gap between the leading vessel and the land. The British ships were so close to each other that Nelson, speaking from his own quarter-deck, was able to ask Hood in the *Zealous*, if he thought they had water enough to round the French line. Hood replied that he had no chart, but would lead and take soundings as he went.

So the British line came on, the men on the yards taking in canvas, the leadsmen in the chains coolly calling the soundings. The battery roared from the island, the leading French ships broke into smoke and flame, but the steady British line glided on. The *Goliath* by this time led; and at half-past five the shadow of its tall masts cast by the westering sun fell over the decks of the *Guerrier*, and as Foley, its captain, swept past the Frenchman's bows, he poured in a furious broadside, bore swiftly up, and dropped—as Nelson, with that minute attention to detail which marks a great commander, had ordered all his captains—an anchor from the stern, so that, without having to "swing," he was instantly in a fighting position on his enemy's quarter. Foley, however, dropped his anchor a moment too late, and drifted on to the second ship in the line; but Hood, in the *Zealous*, coming swiftly after, also raked the *Guerrier*, and, anchoring from the stern at the exact moment, took the place on its quarter Foley should have taken.

The *Orion* came into battle next, blasted the unfortunate *Guerrier*, whose foremast had already gone, with a third broadside, and swept outside the *Zealous* and *Goliath* down to the third ship on the French line. A French frigate, the *Sérieuse*, of thirty-six guns, anchored inside the French line, ventured to fire on the *Orion* as it swept past, whereupon Saumarez, its commander, discharged his starboard broadside into that frigate. The *Sérieuse* reeled under the shock of the British guns, its masts disappeared like chips, and the unfortunate Frenchman went down like a stone; while Saumarez, laying himself on the larboard bow of the *Franklin* and the quarter of the *Peuple Sovrain*, broke upon them in thunder. The *Theseus* followed hard in the track of the *Orion*, raked the unhappy *Guerrier* in the familiar fashion while crossing its bows, then swept through the narrow water-lane betwixt the *Goliath* and *Zealous* and their French

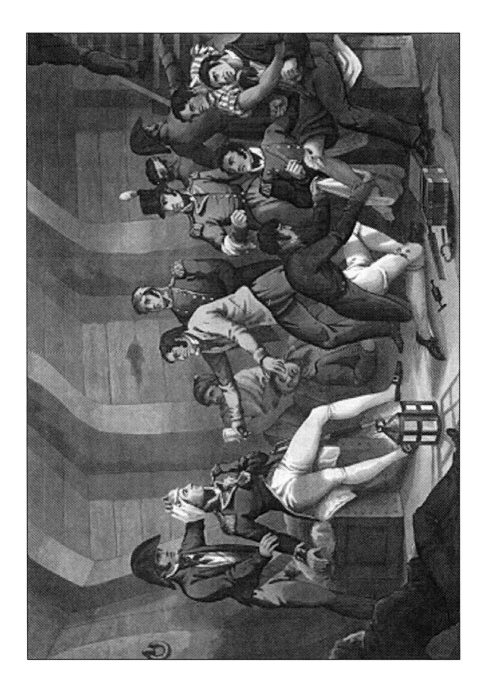

antagonists, poured a smashing broadside into each French ship as it passed, then shot outside the *Orion*, and anchored with mathematical nicety off the quarter of the *Spartiate*. The water-lane was not a pistol-shot wide, and this feat of seamanship was marvellous.

Miller, who commanded the *Theseus*, in a letter to his wife described the fight. "In running along the enemy's line in the wake of the *Zealous* and *Goliath*, I observed," he says, "their shot sweep just over us, and knowing well that at such a moment Frenchmen would not have coolness enough to change their elevation, I closed them suddenly, and, running under the arch of their shot, reserved my fire, every gun being loaded with two, and some with three round shot, until I had the *Guerrier 's* masts in a line, and her jib-boom about six feet clear of our rigging. We then opened with such effect that a second breath could not be drawn before her main and mizzen-mast were also gone. This was precisely at sunset, or forty-four minutes past six."

The *Audacious*, meanwhile, was too impatient to tack round the head of the French line; it broke through the gap betwixt the first and second ships of the enemy, delivered itself, in a comfortable manner, of a raking broadside into both as it passed, took its position on the larboard bow of the *Conquerant*, and gave itself up to the joy of battle. Within thirty minutes from the beginning of the fight, that is, five British line-of-battle ships were inside the French line, comfortably established on the bows or quarters of the leading ships. Nelson himself, in the *Vanguard*, anchored on the outside of the French line, within eighty yards of the *Spartiate's* starboard beam; the *Minotaur*, the *Bellerophon*, and the *Majestic*, coming up in swift succession, and at less than five minutes' interval from each other, flung themselves on the next ships.

How the thunder of the battle deepened, and how the quick flashes of the guns grew brighter as the night gathered rapidly over sea, must be imagined. But Nelson's swift and brilliant strategy was triumphant. Each ship in the French van resembled nothing so much as a walnut in the jaws of a nut-cracker. They were being "cracked" in succession, and the rear of the line could only look on with agitated feel-ings and watch the operation.

The fire of the British ships for fury and precision was overwhelming. The head of the *Guerrier* was simply shot away; the anchors hanging from her bows were cut in two; her main-deck ports, from the bowsprit to the gangway, were driven into one; her masts, fallen inboard, lay with their tangle of rigging on the unhappy crew; while some of her main-deck beams—all supports being torn away—fell on the guns. Hood, in the *Zealous*, who was pounding the unfortunate *Guerrier*, says, "At last, being tired of kill-ing men in that way, I sent a lieutenant on board, who was allowed, as I had instructed him, to hoist a light, and haul it down as a sign of submission." But all the damage was not on the side of the French. The great French flagship, the *Orient*, by this time had added her mighty voice to the tumult, and the *Bellerophon*, who was engaged with her, had a bad time of it. It was the story of Tom Sayers and Heenan over again—a dwarf fighting a giant. Her mizzen-mast and mainmast were shot away, and after maintaining the dread-ful duel for more than an hour, and having 200 of her crew struck down, at 8.20 p.m. the *Bellerophon* cut her cable and drifted, a disabled wreck, out of the fire.

Meanwhile the four ships Nelson had left in the offing were beating furiously up to add themselves to the fight. Night had fallen, by the time Troubridge, in the *Culloden*, came round the island; and then, in full sight of the great battle, the *Culloden* ran hopelessly ashore! She was, perhaps, the finest ship of the British fleet, and the emotions of its crew and commander as they listened to the tumult, and watched through the darkness the darting fires of the Titanic combat they could not share, may be imagined. "Our army," according to well-known authorities, "swore terribly in Flanders." The expletives discharged that night along the decks and in the forecastle of the *Culloden* would probably have made even a Flanders veteran open his eyes in astonishment.

The *Swiftsure* and the *Alexander*, taking warning by the *Culloden's* fate, swept round her and bore safely up to the fight. The *Swiftsure*, bearing down through the darkness to the combat, came across a vessel drifting, dismasted and lightless, a mere wreck. Holliwell, the captain of the *Swiftsure*, was about to fire, thinking it was an enemy, but on second thoughts hailed instead, and got for an answer the words, "*Bellerophon*; going out of action, disabled." The *Swiftsure* passed on, and five minutes after the *Bellerophon* had drifted from the bows of the *Orient* the *Swiftsure*, coming mysteriously up out of the darkness, took her place, and broke into a tempest of fire.

At nine o'clock the great French flagship burst into flame. The painters had been at work upon her on the morning of that day, and had left oil and combustibles about. The nearest English ships concentrated their fire, both of musketry and of cannon, on the burning patch, and made the task of extinguishing it hopeless. Bruéys, the French admiral, had already been cut in two by a cannon shot, and Casablanca, his commodore, was wounded. The fire spread, the flames leaped up the masts and crept athwart the decks of the great ship. The moon had just risen, and the whole scene was perhaps the strangest ever witnessed—the great burning ship, the white light of the moon above, the darting points of red flame from the iron lips of hundreds of guns below, the drifting battle-smoke, the cries of ten thousand combatants—all crowded into an area of a few hundred square yards!

The British ships, hanging like limmids on the flanks of the *Orient*, knew that the explosion might come at any moment, and they made every preparation for it, closing their hatchways, and gathering their firemen at quarters. But they would not withdraw their ships a single yard! At ten o'clock the great French ship blew up with a flame that for a moment lit shore and sea, and a sound that hushed into stillness the whole tumult of the battle. Out of a crew of over a thousand men only seventy were saved! For ten minutes after that dreadful sight the warring fleets seemed stupefied. Not a shout was heard, not a shot fired. Then the French ship next the missing flagship broke into wrathful fire, and the battle awoke in full passion once more.

The fighting raged with partial intermissions all through the night, and when morning broke Bruéys' curved line of mighty battleships, a mile and a half long, had vanished. Of the French ships, one had been blown up, one was sunk, one was ashore, four had fled, the rest were prizes. It was the most complete and dramatic victory in naval history. The French fought on the whole with magnificent courage; but, though stronger in the mass, Nelson's strategy and the seamanship of his captains made the British stronger at every point of actual battle. The rear of the French line did not fire a shot or lose a man. The wonder is that when Nelson's strategy was developed, and its fatal character un-

derstood, Villeneuve, who commanded the French rear, and was a man of undoubted courage, did not cut his cables, make sail, and come to the help of his comrades. A few hundred yards would have carried him to the heart of the fight. Can any one doubt whether, if the positions had been reversed, Nelson would have watched the destruction of half his fleet as a mere spectator? If nothing better had offered, he would have pulled in a wash-tub into the fight!

Villeneuve afterwards offered three explanations of his own inertness—(1) he "could not spare any of his anchors"; (2) "he had no instructions"! (3) "on board the ships in the rear the idea of weighing and going to the help of the ships engaged occurred to no one"! In justice to the French, however, it may be admitted that nothing could surpass the fierceness and valour with which, say, the *Tonnant* was fought. Its captain, Du Petit-Thouars, fought his ship magnificently, had first both his arms and then one of his legs shot away, and died entreating his officers not to strike. Of the ten French ships engaged, the captains of eight were killed or wounded. Nelson took the seven wounded captains on board the *Vanguard*, and, as they recovered, they dined regularly with him. One of the captains had lost his nose, another an eye, another most of his teeth, with musket-shots, &c. Nelson, who himself had been wounded, and was still half-blind as a result, at one of his dinners offered by mischance a case of toothpicks to the captain on his left, who had lost all his teeth. He discovered his error, and in his confusion handed his snuff-box to the captain on his right, who had lost his nose!

What was the secret of the British victory? Nelson's brilliant strategy was only possible by virtue of the magnificent seamanship of his captains, and the new fashion of

51

close and desperate fighting, which Hood and Jarvis and Nelson himself had created. It is a French writer, Captain Gravière, who says that the French naval habit of evading battle where they could, and of accepting action from an enemy rather than forcing it upon him, had ruined the *morale* of the French navy. The long blockades had made Nelson's captains perfect seamen, and he taught them that close fighting at a pistol-shot distance was the secret of victory. "No English captain," he said, "can do wrong who, in fight, lays a ship alongside an enemy." It was a captain of Nelson's school—a Scotchman—who at Camperdown, unable, just as the action began, to read some complicated signal from his chief, flung his signal-book on the deck, and in broad Scotch exclaimed, "D—— me! up with the hellem an' gang in the middle o't." That trick of "ganging into the middle o't" was irresistible.

The battle of the Nile destroyed the naval prestige of France, made England supreme in the Mediterranean, saved India, left Napoleon and his army practically prisoners in Egypt, and united Austria, Russia, and Turkey in league against France. The night battle in Aboukir Bay, in a word, changed the face of history.

CHAPTER 4

The Night Attack off Cadiz

On the morning of July 3, 1801, a curious scene, which might almost be described as a sea comedy, was being transacted off the coast of Alicante. Three huge French line-of-battle ships were manoeuvring and firing round a tiny little British brig-of-war. It was like three mastiffs worrying a mouse. The brig was Lord Cochrane's famous little *Speedy*, a craft so tiny that its commander could carry its entire broadside in his own pockets, and when he shaved himself in his cabin, had to put his head through the skylight and his shaving-box on the quarter-deck, in order to stand upright.

Cochrane was caught by Admiral Linois' squadron, consisting of two ships of eighty guns and one of seventy-four, on a lee shore, where escape was impossible; but from four o'clock till nine o'clock Cochrane evaded all the efforts of his big pursuers to capture him. The French ships separated on different tacks, so as to keep the little *Speedy* constantly under the fire of one or the other; and as the British brig turned and dashed at one opening of the moving triangle or the other, the great ships thundered their broadsides at her. Cochrane threw his guns and stores overboard, and by the most ingenious seamanship evaded capture for hours, surviving some scores of broadsides. He could tack far more quickly than the gigantic ships that pursued him, and again and again the *Speedy* spun round on its heel and shot off on a new course, leaving its particular pursuer with sheet shivering, and nothing but space to fire into. Once, by a quick turn, he shot past one of the 80-gun ships occupied in trying to tack, and got clear. The *Desaix*, however, a seventy-four, was swiftly on the track of the *Speedy*; its tall canvas under the growing breeze give it an advantage, and it ran down to within musket-shot of the *Speedy*, then yawed, bringing its whole broadside to bear, intending to sink its tiny foe with a single discharge. In yawing, however, the *Desaix* shot a little too far, and the weight of her broadside only smote the water, but the scattered grape cut up the *Speedy's* rigging and canvas so terribly that nothing was left but surrender.

When Cochrane went on board his captor, its gallant captain refused to take his sword, saying he "could not accept the sword of an officer who had struggled for so many hours against impossibility." Cochrane and his gallant crew were summarily packed into the Frenchman's hold, and when the French in their turn were pursued by the British line-of-battle ships, as every broadside crashed on the hull of the ship that held them captive, Cochrane and his men gave a round of exultant cheers, until the exasperated Frenchmen threatened to shoot them unless they would hold their tongues—an announcement which only made the British sailors cheer a little louder. The fight between Saumarez and Linois ended with a tragedy; but it may be said to have begun with a farce.

The presence of a French squadron in the Straits of Gibraltar at this particular moment may be explained in a few sentences. Napoleon had woven afresh the web of those naval "combinations" so often torn to fragments by British seamanship and daring. He had persuaded or bullied Spain into placing under the French flag a squadron of six line-of-battle ships, including two leviathans of 112 guns each, lying in the harbour of Cadiz. With haughty, it might almost be said with insolent daring, a couple of British seventy-fours—sometimes, indeed, only one—patrolled the entrance to Cadiz, and blockaded a squadron of ten times their own force. Napoleon's plan was to draw a strong French squadron, under Admiral Linois, from Toulon, a second Spanish squadron from Ferrol, unite these with the ships lying in Cadiz, and thus form a powerful fleet of at least fifteen ships of the line, with a garnishing of frigates.

Once having got his fleet, Napoleon's imagination—which had a strong predatory bias—hesitated betwixt two uses to which it could be turned. One was to make a dash on Lisbon, and require, under threat of an instant bombardment, the delivery of all British ships and goods lying there. This ingenious plan, it was reckoned, would fill French pockets with cash and adorn French brows with glory at one stroke. The amount of British booty at Lisbon was computed—somewhat airily—at 200,000,000 pounds; its disappearance would send half the mercantile houses of Great Britain into the insolvency court, and, to quote a French state paper on the subject, "our fleet, without being buffeted about the sea, would return to Brest loaded with riches and covered with glory, and France would once more astonish Europe." The alternative scheme was to transport some 32,000 new troops to Egypt and restore French fortunes in that country.

Meanwhile Great Britain took energetic measures to wreck this new combination. Sir James Saumarez, in the

Caesar, of eighty guns, with six seventy-fours, was despatched
to keep guard over Cadiz; and he had scarcely reached his
station there when a boat, pulling furiously over from Gibraltar, reported that Admiral Linois' squadron had made its
appearance off the Rock, beating up westward. The sails of
the *Caesar* were instantly swung round, a many-coloured
flutter of bunting summoned the rest of the squadron to
follow, and Saumarez began his eager chase of the French,
bearing away for the Gut under a light north-west wind.
But the breeze died down, and the current swept the straggling ships westward. All day they drifted helplessly, and the
night only brought a breath of air sufficient to fan them
through the Straits.

Meanwhile Linois had taken refuge in the tiny curve
of the Spanish coast known as the roadstead of Algeciras.
Linois was, perhaps, the best French seaman of his day, having, it is true, very little French dash, but endowed with a
wealth of cool resolution, and a genius for defensive warfare
altogether admirable. Algeciras gave Linois exactly what he
wanted, an almost unassailable position. The roadstead is
open, shallow, and plentifully besprinkled with rocks, while
powerful shore batteries covered the whole anchorage with
their zone of fire. The French admiral anchored his ships at
intervals of 500 yards from each other, and so that the lines
of fire from the batteries north and south crossed in front of
his ships. The French squadron carried some 3000 troops,
and these were at once landed, and, manning the batteries,
raised them to a high degree of effectiveness. Some fourteen
heavy Spanish gunboats added enormously to the strength
of the French position.

The French never doubted that Saumarez would instantly
attack; the precedents of the Nile and of Copenhagen were

too recent to make any doubt possible. And Saumarez did
exactly what his enemies expected. Algeciras, in fact, is the
battle of the Nile in miniature. But Saumarez, though he
had the swift daring of Nelson, lacked his warlike genius.
Nelson, in Aboukir Bay, leaped without an instant's pause
on the line of his enemy, but then he had his own ships
perfectly in hand, and so made the leap effective. Saumarez sent his ships into the fight headlong, and without the
least regard to mutual support. At 7.50 on the morning of
July 6, an uncertain gust of air carried the leading British
ship, the *Pompée*, round Cabrita; Hood, in the *Venerable*, lay
becalmed in the offing; the flagship, with the rest of the
squadron, were mere pyramids of idle canvas on the rim
of the horizon.

The *Pompée* drifted down the whole French line, scorched
with the fire of batteries and of gunboats, as well as by the
broadsides of the great French ships, and at 8.45 dropped
her anchor so close to the *Formidable*—a ship much bigger
than itself—that the Frenchman's buoy lay outside her. Then,
deliberately clewing up her sails and tautening her springs,
the *Pompée* opened a fire on her big antagonist so fierce,
sustained, and deadly, that the latter found it intolerable, and
began to warp closer to the shore. The *Audacious* and *Venerable* came slowly up into their assigned positions, and here
was a spectacle of three British ships fighting four French
ships and fourteen Spanish gunboats, with heavy shore batteries manned by 3000 troops thrown into the scale! At this
stage, too, the *Pompée's* springs gave way, or were shot away,
the current swung her round till she lay head on to the
broadside of her huge antagonist, while the batteries smote
her with a deadly cross-fire. A little after ten o'clock the
Caesar dropped anchor three cables' lengths from the *In-*

domptable, and opened a fire which the French themselves described as "tremendous" upon her antagonist.

Linois found the British fire too destructive, and signalled his ships to cut or slip their cables, calculating that a faint air from the sea, which was beginning to blow, would drift them closer under the shelter of the batteries. Saumarez, too, noticed that his topsails were beginning to swell, and he instantly slipped his cable and endeavoured to close with the *Indomptable*, signalling his ships to do the same. The British cables rattled hoarsely through their hawse-holes along the whole line, and the ships were adrift; but the breeze almost instantly died away, and on the strong coast current the British ships floated helplessly, while the fire from the great shore batteries, and from the steady French decks, now anchored afresh, smote them heavily in turn. The *Pompée* lay for an hour under a concentrated fire without being able to bring a gun to bear in return, and then summoned by signal the boats of the squadron to tow her off.

Saumarez, meanwhile, had ordered the *Hannibal*, under Captain Ferris, to round the head of the French line and "rake the admiral's ship." Ferris, by fine seamanship, partly sailed and partly drifted into the post assigned to him, and then grounded hopelessly, under a plunging fire from the shore batteries, within hail of the Frenchman, itself also aground. A fire so dreadful soon reduced the unfortunate *Hannibal* to a state of wreck. Boats from the *Caesar* and the *Venerable* came to her help, but Ferris sent them back again. They could not help him, and should not share his fate. Saumarez, as a last resource, prepared for a boat attack on the batteries, but in the whole squadron there were not enough uninjured boats to carry the marines. The British

flagship itself was by this time well nigh a wreck, and was drifting on the reefs. A flaw of wind from the shore gave the ships steerage-way, and Saumarez drew off, leaving the *Hannibal* to its fate.

Ferris fought till his masts were gone, his guns dismounted, his bulwarks riddled, his decks pierced, and one-third of his crew killed or wounded. Then he ordered the survivors to the lower decks, and still kept his flag flying for half-an-hour after the shot-torn sails of the shattered British ships had disappeared round Cabrita. Then he struck. Here was a French triumph, indeed! A British squadron beaten off, a British seventy-four captured! It is said that when the news reached Paris the city went half-mad with exultation. Napoleon read the despatch to his ministers with eyes that danced, and almost wept, with mere gladness!

The British squadron—officers and men in such a mood as may be imagined—put into Gibraltar to refit; the *Caesar*, with her mainmast shot through in five places, her boats destroyed, her hull pierced; while of the sorely battered *Pompée* it is recorded that she had "not a mast, yard-spar, shroud, rope, or sail" which was not damaged by hostile shot. Linois, meanwhile, got his grounded ships and his solitary prize afloat, and summoned the Cadiz squadron to join him. On the 9th these ships—six sail of the line, two of them giants of 112 guns each, with three frigates—went triumphantly, with widespread canvas and many-coloured bunting, past Gibraltar, where the shattered British squadron was lying, and cast anchor beside Admiral Linois in Algeciras Bay.

The British were labouring, meanwhile, with fierce energy, to refit their damaged ships under shelter of the guns of Gibraltar. The *Pompée* was practically destroyed, and her crew were distributed amongst the other ships. Saumarez himself regarded the condition of his flagship as hopeless, but his captain, Brenton, begged permission to at least attempt to refit her. He summoned his crew aft, and told the men the admiral proposed to leave the ship behind, and asked them "what they thought about it." The men gave a wrathful roar, punctuated, it is to be feared, with many sea-going explosives, and shouted "All hands to work day and night till she's ready!" The whole crew, down to the very powder-boys, actually worked while daylight lasted, kept it up, watch and watch, through the night, and did this from the evening of the 6th to the noon of the 12th! Probably no ship that ever floated was refitted in shorter time. In that brief period, to quote the "Naval Register," she "shifted her mainmast; fished and secured her foremast, shot through in several places; knotted and spliced the rigging, which had been cut to pieces, and bent new sails; plugged the shot-holes between wind and water; completed with stores of all kinds, anchors and cables, powder and shot, and provisions for four months."

On Sunday, July 12, 1801, the French and Spanish ships in Algeciras Bay weighed anchor, formed their line of battle as they came out, off Cabrita Point, and, stately and slow, with the two 112-gun Spaniards as a rearguard, bore up for Cadiz. An hour later the British ships warped out of the mole in pursuit. It was an amazing sight: a squadron of five sail of the line, which had been completely disabled in an action only five days before, was starting, fresh and refitted, in pursuit of a fleet double its own number, and more than double its strength! All Gibraltar crowded to watch the ships as, one by one, they cleared the pier-head. The garrison band blew itself hoarse playing

"Britons, strike home," while the *Caesar's* band answered in strains as shrill with "Come, cheer up, my lads, 'tis for glory we steer." Both tunes, it may be added, were simply submerged beneath the cheers which rang up from mole-head and batteries and dock-walls. Just as the *Caesar* drifted, huge and stately, past the pier-head, a boat came eagerly pulling up to her. It was crowded with jack-tars, with bandaged heads and swathed arms. A cluster of the *Pompée's* wounded, who escaped from the hospital, bribed a boatman to pull them out to the flagship, and clamoured to be taken on board!

Saumarez had strengthened his squadron by the addition of the *Superb*, with the *Thames* frigate, and at twenty minutes to nine P.M., vainly searching the black horizon for the lights of the enemy, he hailed the *Superb*, and ordered its captain, Keats, to clap on all sail and attack the enemy directly he overtook them. Saumarez, in a word, launched a single seventy-four against a fleet! Keats was a daring sailor; his ship was, perhaps, the fastest British seventy-four afloat, and his men were instantly aloft spreading every inch of canvas. Then, like a huge ghost, the *Superb* glided ahead and vanished in the darkness. The wind freshened; the blackness deepened; the lights of the British squadron died out astern. But a wide sprinkle of lights ahead became visible; it was the Spanish fleet! Eagerly the daring *Superb* pressed on, with slanting decks and men at quarters, but with lights hidden. At midnight the rear ships of the Spanish squadron were under the larboard bow of the *Superb*—two stupendous three-deckers, with lights gleaming through a hundred port-holes—while a French two-decker to larboard of both the Spanish giants completed the line.

Keats, unseen and unsuspected, edged down with his solitary seventy-four, her heaviest guns only 18-pounders, on the quarter of the nearest three-decker. He was about to fling himself, in the gloom of the night, on three great ships, with an average of 100 guns each! Was ever a more daring feat attempted? Silently through the darkness the *Superb* crept, her canvas glimmering ghostly white, till she was within some 200 yards of the nearest Spaniard. Then out of the darkness to windward there broke on the astonished and drowsy Spaniards a tempest of flame, a whirlwind of shot. Thrice the *Superb* poured her broadside into the huge and staggering bulk of her antagonist. With the second broadside the Spaniard's topmast came tumbling down; with the third, so close was the flame of the *Superb's* guns, the Spanish sails—dry as touch-wood with lying for so many months in the sunshine of Cadiz—took fire.

Meanwhile a dramatic incident occurred. The two great Spaniards commenced to thunder their heavy broadsides into each other! Many of the Superb's shots had struck the second and more distant three-decker. Cochrane, indeed, says that the *Superb* passed actually betwixt the two gigantic Spaniards, fired a broadside, larboard and starboard, into both, and then glided on and vanished in the darkness. It is certain that the *San Hermenegildo*, finding her decks torn by a hurricane of shot, commenced to fire furiously through the smoke and the night at the nearest lights. They were the lights of her own consort! She, in turn, fired at the flash of the guns tormenting her. So, under the black midnight skies, the two great Spanish ships thundered at each other, flame answering flame. They drifted ever closer. The fire of the *Real Carlos* kindled the sails of the sister ship; the flames leaped and danced to the very mast-heads; and, still engaged in a fiery wrestle, they blew up in succession, and out of their united crews of 2000 men only a little over 200 were picked up!

The *Superb*, meanwhile, had glided ahead, leaving the three-deckers to destroy each other, and opened fire at pistol-shot distance on the French two-decker, and in thirty minutes compelled her to strike. In less than two hours of a night action, that is, this single English seventy-four had destroyed two Spanish three-deckers of 112 guns each, and captured a fine French battle-ship of 74 guns!

The British ships by this time were coming up in the rear, with every inch of canvas spread. They swept past the amazing spectacle of the two great Spaniards destroying each other, and pressed on in chase of the enemy. The wind rose to a gale. In the grey dawn the *Caesar* found herself, with all her sister ships, far astern, except the *Venerable*, under Hood, which was hanging on the quarter of the rearmost French ship, the *Formidable*, a magnificent ship of 80 guns, with a gallant commander, and carrying quite too heavy metal for Hood. Hood, however, the most daring of men, exchanged broadsides at pistol-shot distance with his big antagonist, till his ship was dismasted, and was drifted by the current on the rocky shoals off San Pedro. The *Caesar* came up in time to enable its disgusted crew to see ship after ship of the flying enemy disappear safely within the sheltering batteries of Cadiz.

CHAPTER 5

The Battle of Copenhagen

"I have been in a hundred and five engagements, but that of today is the most terrible of them all."This was how Nelson himself summed up the great fight off Copenhagen, or the battle of the Baltic as it is sometimes called, fought on April 2, 1801. It was a battle betwixt Britons and Danes. The men who fought under the blood-red flag of Great Britain, and under the split flag of Denmark with its white cross, were alike the descendants of the Vikings. The blood of the old sea-rovers ran hot and fierce in their veins. Nelson, with the glories of the Nile still ringing about his name, commanded the British fleet, and the fire of his eager and gallant spirit ran from ship to ship like so many volts of electricity. But the Danes fought in sight of their capital, under the eyes of their wives and children. It is not strange that through the four hours during which the thunder of the great battle rolled over the roofs of Copenhagen and up the narrow waters of the Sound, human valour and endurance in both fleets were at their very highest.

What was it in 1801 which sent a British fleet on an errand of battle to Copenhagen?

It was a tiny episode of the long and stern drama of the Napoleonic wars. Great Britain was supreme on the sea, Napoleon on the land, and, in his own words, Na-

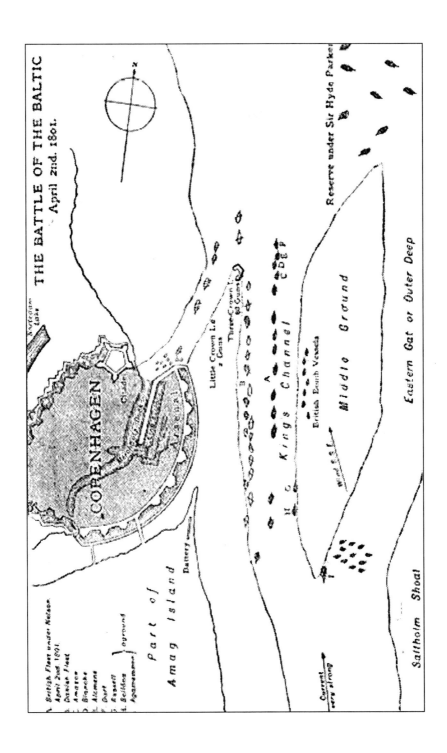

THE BATTLE OF THE BALTIC
April 2nd. 1801.

Part of
Amag Island

COPENHAGEN

Little Crown Ld.
& Guns

Three Crown Ld.
88 Guns

H. C. Kings Channel

CDE F

Middle Ground

Eastern Gat or Outer Deep

Sattholm Shoal

British Batteries Vessels

Wind. E.S.E.

Current
very strong

Reserve under Sir Hyde Parker

Battery

1. British Fleet under Nelson.
   April 2nd 1801.
2. Danish Fleet.
   A. Amarer
   B. Bianche
   C. Alcmene
   D. Dart
   E. Russell
   F. Bellona
   Agamemnon } aground

poleon conceived the idea of "conquering the sea by the land." Paul I. of Russia, a semi-lunatic, became Napoleon's ally and tool. Paul was able to put overwhelming pressure on Sweden, Denmark, and Prussia, and these Powers were federated as the "League of Armed Neutrality," with the avowed purpose of challenging the marine supremacy of Great Britain. Paul seized all British ships in Russian ports; Prussia marched troops into Hanover; every port from the North Cape to Gibraltar was shut against the British flag. Britain, stood alone, practically threatened with a naval combination of all the Northern Powers, while behind the combination stood Napoleon, the subtlest brain and most imperious will ever devoted to the service of war. Napoleon's master passion, it should be remembered, was the desire to overthrow Great Britain, and he held in the palm of his hand the whole military strength of the Continent. The fleets of France and Spain were crushed or blockaded: but the three Northern Powers could have put into battle-line a fleet of fifty great ships and twenty-five frigates. With this force they could raise the blockade of the French ports, sweep triumphant through the narrow seas, and land a French army in Kent or in Ulster.

Pitt was Prime Minister, and his masterful intellect controlled British policy. He determined that the fleets of Denmark and of Russia should not become a weapon in the hand of Napoleon against England; and a fleet of eighteen ships of the line, with frigates and bomb-vessels, was despatched to reason, from the iron lips of their guns, with the misguided Danish Government. Sir Hyde Parker, a decent, unenterprising veteran, was commander-in-chief by virtue of seniority; but Nelson, with the nominal rank of second in command, was the brain and soul of the expedition. "Almost all the safety and certainly all the honour of England," he said to his chief, "is more entrusted to you than ever yet fell to the lot of a British officer." And all through the story of the expedition it is amusing to notice the fashion in which Nelson's fiery nature strove to kindle poor Sir Hyde Barker's sluggish temper to its own flame.

The fleet sailed from Yarmouth on March 12, and fought its way through fierce spring gales to the entrance of the Kattegat. The wind was fair; Nelson was eager to sweep down on Copenhagen with the whole fleet, and negotiate with the whole skyline of Copenhagen crowded with British topsails. "While the negotiation is going on," he said, "the Dane should see our flag waving every time he lifts up his head." Time was worth more than gold; it was worth brave men's lives. The Danes were toiling day and night to prepare the defence of their capital. But prim Sir Hyde anchored, and sent up a single frigate with his ultimatum, and it was not until March 30 that the British fleet, a long line of stately vessels, came sailing up the Sound, passed Elsinore, and cast anchor fifteen miles from Copenhagen. Nothing could surpass the gallant energy shown by the Danes in their preparation for defence, and Nature had done much to make the city impregnable from the sea.

The Sound is narrow and shallow, a mere tangle of shoals wrinkled with twisted channels and scoured by the swift tides. King's Channel runs straight up towards the city, but a huge sandbank, like the point of a toe, splits the channel into two just as it reaches the harbour. The western edge runs up, pocket-shaped, into the city, and forms the actual port; the main channel contracts, swings round to the south-east, and forms a narrow passage between the shallows in front of the city and a huge shoal called the Middle Ground. A cluster of grim and heavily armed fortifications called the Three-Crown Batteries guarded the entrance to the harbour, and looked right up King's Channel; a stretch of floating batteries and line-of-battle ships, a mile and a half in extent, ran from the Three-Crown Batteries along the edge of the shoals in front of the city, with some heavy pile batteries at its termination. The direct approach up King's Channel, together with the narrow passage between the city and the Middle Ground, were thus commanded by the fire of over 600 heavy guns. The Danes had removed the buoys that marked all the channels, the British had no charts, and only the most daring and skilful seamanship could bring the great ships of the British fleet through that treacherous tangle of shoals to the Danish front. As a matter of fact, the heavier ships in the British fleet never attempted to join in the desperate fight which was waged, but hung as mere spectators in the offing.

Meanwhile popular enthusiasm in the Danish capital was at fever-point. Ten thousand disciplined troops manned the batteries; but peasants from the farms, workmen from the factories, merchants from the city, hastened to volunteer, and worked day and night at gun-drill. A thousand students from the university enrolled themselves, and drilled from morning till night. These student-soldiers had probably the best military band ever known; it consisted of the entire orchestra of the Theatre Royal, all volunteers. A Danish officer, sent on some message under a flag of truce to the British fleet, was required to put his message in writing, and was offered a somewhat damaged pen for that purpose. He threw it down with a laugh, saying that "if the British guns were not better pointed than their pens they wouldn't

make much impression on Copenhagen." That flash of gallant wit marked the temper of the Danes. They were on flame with confident daring.

Nelson, always keen for a daring policy, had undertaken to attack the Danish defences with a squadron of twelve seventy-fours, and the frigates and bomb-vessels of the fleet. He determined to shun the open way of King's Channel, grope through the uncertain passage called the Dutch Deep, at the back of the Middle Ground, and forcing his way up the narrow channel in front of the shallows, repeat on the anchored batteries and battleships of the Danes the exploit of the Nile. He spent the nights of March 30 and 31 sounding the channel, being himself, in spite of fog and ice, in the boat nearly the whole of these two bitter nights. On April 1 the fleet came slowly up the Dutch Deep, and dropped anchor at night about two miles from the southern extremity of the Danish line. At eleven o'clock that night, Hardy—in whose arms Nelson afterwards died on board the *Victory*—pushed off from the flagship in a small boat and sounded the channel in front of the Danish floating batteries. So daring was he that he actually sounded round the leading ship of the Danish line, using a pole to avoid being detected.

In the morning the wind blew fair for the channel. Nelson's plans had been elaborated to their minutest details, and the pilots of the fleet were summoned at nine o'clock to the flagship to receive their last instructions. But their nerve failed them. They were simply the mates or masters of Baltic traders turned for the moment into naval pilots. They had no charts. They were accustomed to handle ships of 200 or 300 tons burden, and the task of steering the great British seventy-fours through the labyrinths of shallows, with the tide running like a mill-race, appalled them. At last Murray, in the *Edgar*, undertook to lead. The signal was made to weigh in succession, and one great ship after another, with its topsails on the caps, rounded the shoulder of the Middle Ground, and in stately procession, the *Edgar* leading, came up the channel.

The leading Danish ships broke into a tempest of fire as the British ships came within range. The *Agamemnon* failed to weather the shoulder of the Middle Ground, and went ignobly ashore, and the scour of the tide kept her fast there, in spite of the most desperate exertions of her crew. The *Bellona*, a pile of white canvas above, a double line of curving batteries below, hugged the Middle Ground too closely, and grounded too; and the *Russell*, following close after her, went ashore in the same manner, with its jib-boom almost touching the *Bellona's* taffrail. One-fourth of Nelson's force was thus practically out of the fight before a British gun was fired. These were the ships, too, intended to sail past the whole Danish line and engage the Three-Crown Batteries. As they were *hors de combat*, the frigates of the squadron, under Riou had to take the place of the seventy-fours.

Meanwhile, Nelson, in the *Elephant*, came following hard on the ill-fated *Russell*. Nelson's orders were that each ship should pass her leader on the starboard side, and had he acted on his own orders, Nelson too would have grounded, with every ship that followed him. The interval betwixt each ship was so narrow that decision had to be instant; and Nelson, judging the water to the larboard of the *Russell* to be deeper, put his helm a-starboard, and so shot past the *Russell* on its larboard beam into the true channel, the whole line following his example. That sudden whirl to starboard of the flagship's helm—a flash of brilliant seamanship—saved the battle.

Ship after ship shot past, and anchored, by a cable astern, in its assigned position. The sullen thunder of the guns rolled from end to end of the long line, the flash of the artillery ran in a dance of flame along the mile and a half of batteries, and some 2000 pieces of artillery, most of them of the heaviest calibre, filled the long Sound with the roar of battle. Nelson loved close fighting, and he anchored within a cable's length of the Danish flagship, the pilots refusing to carry the ship nearer on account of the shallow depth, and the average distance of the hostile lines was less than a hundred fathoms. The cannonade raged, deep-voiced, unbroken, and terrible, for three hours. "Warm work," said Nelson, as it seemed to deepen in fury and volume, "but, mark you, I would not be elsewhere for thousands." The carnage was terrific. Twice the Danish flagship took fire, and out of a crew of 336 no fewer than 270 were dead or wounded. Two of the Danish prams drifted from the line, mere wrecks, with cordage in rags, bulwarks riddled, guns dismounted, and decks veritable shambles.

The battle, it must be remembered, raged within easy sight of the city, and roofs and church towers were crowded with spectators. They could see nothing but a low-lying continent of whirling smoke, shaken with the tumult of battle, and scored perpetually, in crimson bars, with the flame of the guns. Above the drifting smoke towered the tops of the British seventy-fours, stately and threatening. The south-east wind presently drove the smoke over the city, and beneath that inky roof, as under the gloom of an eclipse, the crowds of Copenhagen, white-faced with excitement, watched the Homeric fight, in which their sons, and brothers, and husbands were perishing.

Nothing could surpass the courage of the Danes. Fresh crews marched fiercely to the floating batteries as these threatened to grow silent by mere slaughter, and, on decks crimson and slippery with the blood of their predecessors, took up the fight. Again and again, after a Danish ship had struck from mere exhaustion, it was manned afresh from the shore, and the fight renewed. The very youngest officer in the Danish navy was a lad of seventeen named Villemoes. He commanded a tiny floating battery of six guns, manned by twenty-four men, and he managed to bring it under the very counter of Nelson's flagship, and fired his guns point-blank into its huge wooden sides. He stuck to his work until the British marines shot down every man of his tiny crew except four. After the battle Nelson begged that young Villemoes might be introduced to him, and told the Danish Crown Prince that a boy so gallant ought to be made an admiral. "If I were to make all my brave officers admirals," was the reply, "I should have no captains or lieutenants left."

The terrific nature of the British fire, as well as the stubbornness of Danish courage, may be judged from the fact that most of the prizes taken in the fight were so absolutely riddled with shot as to have to be destroyed. Foley, who led the van at the battle of the Nile, was Nelson's flag-captain in the *Elephant*, and he declared he burned fifty more barrels of powder in the four hours' furious cannonade at Copenhagen than he did during the long night struggle at the Nile! The fire of the Danes, it may be added, was almost as obstinate and deadly. The *Monarch*, for example, had no fewer than 210 of its crew lying dead or wounded on its decks. At one o'clock Sir Hyde Parker, who was watching the struggle with a squadron of eight of his heaviest ships from the offing, hoisted a signal to discontinue the engagement. Then came the incident which every boy remembers.

The signal-lieutenant of the *Elephant* reported that the admiral had thrown out No. 39, the signal to discontinue the fight. Nelson was pacing his quarterdeck fiercely, and took no notice of the report. The signal-officer met him at the next turn, and asked if he should repeat the signal. Nelson's reply was to ask if his own signal for close action was still hoisted.

"Yes," said the officer.

"Mind you keep it so," said Nelson. Nelson continued to tramp his quarter-deck, the thunder of the battle all about him, his ship reeling to the recoil of its own guns. The stump of his lost arm jerked angrily to and fro, a sure sign of excitement with him. "Leave off action!" he said to his lieutenant; "I'm hanged if I do. You know, Foley," he said, turning to his captain, "I've only one eye; I've a right to be blind sometimes." And then putting the glass to his blind eye, he exclaimed, "I really do not see the signal!" He dismissed the incident by saying, "D—— the signal! Keep mine for closer action flying!"

As a matter of fact, Parker had hoisted the signal only to give Nelson the opportunity for withdrawing from the fight if he wished. The signal had one disastrous result—the little cluster of frigates and sloops engaged with the Three-Crown Batteries obeyed it and hauled off. As the *Amazon*, Riou's ship, ceased to fire, the smoke lifted, and the Danish battery got her in full sight, and smote her with deadly effect. Riou himself, heartbroken with having to abandon the fight, had just exclaimed, "What will Nelson think of us!" when a chain-shot cut him in two, and with him a sailor with something of Nelson's own genius for battle perished.

By two o'clock the Danish fire began to slack. One-half the line was a mere chain of wrecks; some of the floating batteries had sunk; the flagship was a mass of flames. Nelson at this point sent his boat ashore with a flag of truce, and a letter to the Prince Regent. The letter was addressed, "To the Danes, the brothers of Englishmen." If the fire continued from the Danish side, Nelson said he would be compelled to set on fire all the floating batteries he had taken, "without being able to save the brave Danes who had defended them." Somebody offered Nelson, when he had written the letter, a wafer with which to close it. "This," said Nelson, "is no time to appear hurried or informal," and he insisted on the letter being carefully sealed with wax. The Crown Prince proposed an armistice. Nelson, with great shrewdness, referred the proposal to his admiral lying four miles off in the *London*, foreseeing that the long pull out and back would give him time to get his own crippled ships clear of the shoals, and past the Three-Crown Batteries into the open channel beyond—the only course the wind made possible; and this was exactly what happened. Nelson, it is clear, was a shrewd diplomatist as well as a great sailor.

The night was coming on black with the threat of tempest; the Danish flagship had just blown up; but the white flag of truce was flying, and the British toiled, as fiercely as they had fought, to float their stranded ships and take possession of their shattered prizes. Of these, only one was found capable of being sufficiently repaired to be taken to

Portsmouth. On the 4th Nelson himself landed and visited the Crown Prince, and a four months' truce was agreed upon. News came at that moment of the assassination of Paul I., and the League of Armed Neutrality—the device by which Napoleon hoped to overthrow the naval power of Great Britain—vanished into mere space. The fire of Nelson's guns at Copenhagen wrecked Napoleon's whole naval policy.

It is curious that, familiar as Nelson was with the grim visage of battle, the carnage of that four hours' cannonade was too much for even his steady nerves. He could find no words too generous to declare his admiration of the obstinate courage shown by the Danes. "The French and Spanish fight well," he said, "but they could not have stood for an hour such a fire as the Danes sustained for four hours."

CHAPTER 7

Trafalgar

1. THE STRATEGY

That Trafalgar was a great British victory, won by splendid seamanship and by magnificent courage, everybody knows. On October 21, 1805, Nelson, with twenty-seven line-of-battle ships, attacked Villeneuve, in command of a combined fleet of thirty-three line-of-battle ships. The first British gun was fired at 12.10 o'clock; at 5 o'clock the battle was over; and within those five hours the combined fleets of France and Spain were simply destroyed. No fewer than eighteen ships of the line were captured, burnt, or sunk; the rest were in flight, and had practically ceased to exist as a fighting force. But what very few people realise is that Trafalgar is only the last incident in a great strategic conflict—a warfare of brains rather than of bullets—which for nearly three years raged round a single point. For that long period the warlike genius of Napoleon was pitted in strategy against the skill and foresight of a cluster of British sailors; and the sailors won. They beat Napoleon at his own weapons. The French were not merely out-fought in the shock of battling fleets, they were out-generalled in the conflict of plotting and warlike brains which preceded the actual fight off Cape Trafalgar.

The strategy which preceded Trafalgar represents Napoleon's solitary attempt to plan a great campaign on the tossing floor of the sea. "It has an interest wholly unique," says Mahan, "as the only great naval campaign ever planned by this foremost captain of modern times." And it is a very marvellous fact that a cluster of British sailors—Jervis and Barham (a salt eighty years old) at the Admiralty, Cornwallis at Brest, Collingwood at Cadiz, and Nelson at Toulon—guessed all Napoleon's profound and carefully hidden strategy, and met it by even subtler plans and swifter resolves than those of Napoleon himself. The five hours of gallant fighting off Cape Trafalgar fill us with exultant pride. But the intellectual duel which preceded the shock of actual battle, and which lasted for nearly three years, is, in a sense, a yet more splendid story. Great Britain may well honour her naval leaders of that day for their cool and profound strategy, as much as for the unyielding courage with which such a blockade as, say, that of Brest by Cornwallis was maintained for years, or such splendid daring as that which Collingwood showed when, in the *Royal Sovereign*, he broke Villeneuve's line at Trafalgar.

When in 1803 the war which brought to an end the brief peace of Amiens broke out, Napoleon framed a great and daring plan for the invasion of England. French plans for the invasion of England were somewhat numerous a century or so ago. The Committee of Public Safety in 1794, while keeping the guillotine busy in the Place de la Révolution, had its own little plan for extending the Reign of Terror, by means of an invasion, to England; and on May 27 of that year solemnly appointed one of their number to represent the Committee in England "when it was conquered." The member chosen was citizen Bon Saint André, the same hero who, in the battle of the 1st of June, fled in terror to the refuge of the French flagship's cock-pit when the *Queen Charlotte*, with her triple lines of guns, came too alarmingly near. But Napoleon's plans for the same object in 1803 were definite, formidable, profound. Great Britain was the one barrier in the path of his ambition. "Buonaparte," says Green, in his "Short History of the English People," "was resolute to be master of the western world, and no medium of popular freedom or sense of popular right ever interfered with his resolve. . . . England was now the one country where freedom in any sense remained alive. . . . With the fall of England, despotism would have been universal throughout Europe; and it was at England that Buonaparte resolved to strike the first blow in his career of conquest. Fifteen millions of people, he argued, must give way to forty millions."

So he formed the vast camp at Boulogne, in which were gathered 130,000 veterans. A great flotilla of boats was built, each boat being armed with one or two guns, and capable of carrying 100 soldiers. More than 1000 of such boats were built, and concentrated along twenty miles of the Channel coast, and at four different ports. A new port was dug at Boulogne, to give shelter to the main division of this flotilla, and great and powerful batteries erected for its protection. The French soldiers were exercised in embarking and disembarking till the whole process could be counted by minutes. "Let us," said Napoleon, "be masters of the Straits for six hours, and we shall be masters of the world."

When since the days of William the Conqueror were the shores of Great Britain menaced by such a peril? "There is no difficulty," said Moltke, "in getting an army into England; the trouble would be to get it out again." And, no doubt, Englishmen, fighting on their own soil and for their own hearths, would have given an invader a very rough time of it. But let it be remembered that Napoleon was a military genius of the first order, and that the 130,000 soldiers waiting on the heights above Boulogne to leap on British soil were, to quote Mahan, "the most brilliant soldiery of all time." They were the men who afterwards won Austerlitz, who struck down Prussia with a single blow at Jena, who marched as victors through the streets of Vienna and of Berlin, and fought their way to Moscow. Imagine such an army, with such a leader, landed on the green fields of Kent! In that case there might have been an English Austerlitz or Friedland. London might have shared the fate of Moscow. If Napoleon had succeeded, the fate of the world would have been changed, and Toronto and Cape Town, Melbourne and Sydney and Auckland might have been ruled by French prefects.

Napoleon himself was confident of success. He would reach London, he calculated, within four days of landing, and then he would have issued decrees abolishing the House of Lords, proclaiming a redistribution of property, and declaring England a republic. "You would never have burned your capital," he said to O'Meara at St. Helena; "you are too rich and fond of money." The London mob, he believed, would have joined him, for, as he cynically argued, "the *canaille* of all nations are nearly alike."

Even Napoleon would probably have failed, however, in subduing Great Britain, and would have remained a prisoner where he came intending to be a conqueror. As he himself said when a prisoner on his way to St. Helena, "I entered into no calculation as to the manner in which I was to return"! But in the battles which must have been fought, how many English cities would have perished in flames, how many English rivers would have run red with the blood of slain men! "At Waterloo," says Alison, "England fought for victory; at Trafalgar for existence."

But "the streak of silver sea" guarded England, and for more than two years Napoleon framed subtle plans and organised vast combinations which might give him that brief six hours' command of the Strait which was all he needed, as he thought, to make himself the master of the world. The flotilla could not so much as get out of the ports, in which the acres of boats lay, in a single tide, and one half of the army of invasion must lie tossing—and, it may be suspected, dreadfully sea-sick—for hours outside these ports, waiting for the other half to get afloat. Then there remained forty miles of sea to cross. And what would happen if, say, Nelson and Collingwood, with a dozen 74-gun ships, got at work amongst the flotilla? It would be a combat between wolves and sheep. It was Nelson's chief aspiration to have the opportunity of "trying Napoleon on a wind," and the attempt to cross the Straits might have given him that chance. All Napoleon's resources and genius were therefore strained to give him for the briefest possible time the command of the Channel; and the skill and energy of the British navy were taxed to the utmost to prevent that consummation.

Now, France, as a matter of fact, had a great fleet, but it was scattered, and lying imprisoned, in fragments, in widely separated ports. There were twelve ships of the line in Toulon, twenty in Brest, five in Rochefort, yet other five in Ferrol; and the problem for Napoleon was, somehow, to set these imprisoned squadrons free, and assemble them for twenty-four hours off Boulogne. The British policy, on the other hand, was to maintain a sleepless blockade of these

ports, and keep the French fleet sealed up in scattered and helpless fragments. The battle for the Straits of Dover, the British naval chiefs held, must be fought off Brest and Ferrol and Toulon; and never in the history of the world were blockades so vigilant, and stern, and sleepless maintained.

Nelson spent two years battling with the fierce northwesters of the Gulf of Lyons, keeping watch over a great French squadron in Toulon, and from May 1803 to August 1805 left his ship only three times, and for less than an hour on each occasion. The watch kept by Cornwallis off Brest, through summer and winter, for nearly three years, Mahan declares, has never, for constancy and vigilance, been excelled, perhaps never equalled, in the history of blockades. The hardship of these long sea-watches was terrible. It was waging an fight with weariness and brain-paralysing monotony, with cold and scurvy and tempest, as well as with human foes. Collingwood was once twenty-two months at sea without dropping anchor. In seventeen years of sea service—between 1793 and 1810—he was only twelve months in England.

The wonder is that the seamen of that day did not grow web-footed, or forget what solid ground felt like! Collingwood tells his wife in one letter that he had "not seen a green leaf on a tree" for fourteen months! By way of compensation, these long and stern blockades developed such a race of seamen as perhaps the world has never seen before or since; exhaustless of resource, hardy, tireless, familiar with every turn of sea life, of iron frame and an iron courage which neither tempest nor battle could shake. Great Britain, as a matter of fact, won her naval battles, not because she had better ships or heavier guns than her enemies, but only because she trained a finer race of seamen. Says

Brenton, himself a gallant sailor of the period, "I have seen Spanish line-of-battle ships twenty-four hours unmooring; as many minutes are sufficient for a well-manned British ship to perform the same operation. When, on any grand ceremony, they found it necessary to cross their top-gallant yards in harbour, they began the day before; we cross ours in one minute from the deck."

But it was those iron-like leaders that in the long-run thwarted the plans of Napoleon and changed the fate of the world. Cornwallis off Brest, Collingwood off Roche-fort, Pellew off Ferrol, Nelson before Toulon, fighting the wild gales of the Bay of Biscay and the fierce north-westers of the Gulf of Lyons, in what Mahan calls "that tremendous and sustained vigilance which reached its utmost tension in the years preceding Trafalgar," really saved England. "Those far-distant, storm-beaten ships, upon which the Grand Army never looked," says Mahan, "stood between it and the dominion of the world."

An intellect so subtle and combative as Napoleon's was, of course, strained to the utmost to break or cheat the British blockades, and the story of the one crafty ruse after another which he employed to beguile the British leaders is very remarkable. Even more remarkable, perhaps, is the manner in which these plain-minded, business-like British seamen, for whose mental powers Napoleon cherished the deepest contempt, fathomed his plans and shattered his combinations.

Napoleon's first plot was decidedly clever. He gathered in Brest 20,000 troops, ostensibly for a descent upon Ireland. This, he calculated, would preoccupy Cornwallis, and prevent him moving. The Toulon fleet was to run out with the first north-west wind, and, as long as a British lookout ship was in sight, would steer east, as though making for Egypt; but when beyond sight of British eyes the fleet was to swing round, run through the Straits, be joined off Cadiz by the Rochefort squadron, and sweep, a great fleet of at least sixteen sail of the line, past the Scilly Islands to Boulogne. Napoleon calculated that Nelson would be racing in the direction of Egypt, Cornwallis would be redoubling his vigilance before Brest, at the exact moment the great Boulogne flotilla was carrying its 130,000 invading Frenchmen to Dover! Napoleon put the one French admiral as to whose resolve and daring he was sure—Latouche Treville—in command of the Toulon fleet; but before the moment for action came Treville died, and Napoleon had to fall back upon a weaker man, Villeneuve.

He changed his plans to suit the qualities of his new admiral—the Toulon and Rochefort squadrons were to break out, sail separately to a rendezvous in the West Indies, and, once joined, spread havoc through the British possessions there. "I think," wrote Napoleon, "that the sailing of these twenty ships of the line will oblige the English to despatch over thirty in pursuit." So the blockades everywhere would be weakened, and the Toulon and Rochefort squadrons, doubling back to Europe, were to raise the blockade off Ferrol and Brest, and the Brest squadron was to land 18,000 troops, under Augereau, in Ireland, while the Grand Army of Boulogne was to cross the Straits, with Napoleon at its head. Thus Great Britain and Ireland would be invaded simultaneously.

The trouble was to set the scheme going by the release of the Toulon and Rochefort squadrons. Nelson's correspondence shows that he guessed Napoleon's strategy. If the Toulon fleet broke loose, he wrote, he was sure its course would be held for the Atlantic, and thither he would follow it. In the meanwhile he kept guard so steadfastly that the great French strategy could not get itself started. In December 1804 war broke out betwixt Britain and Spain, and this gave Napoleon a new ally and a new fleet. Napoleon found he had nearly sixty line-of-battle ships, French or Spanish, to weave into his combinations, and he framed— to use Mahan's words—"upon lines equal, both in boldness and scope, to those of the Marengo and Austerlitz campaigns, the immense strategy which resulted in Trafalgar." The Toulon and Rochefort squadrons, as before, were to break out separately, rendezvous in the West Indies, return by a different route to European waters, pick up the French and Spanish ships in Ferrol, and then sweep through the narrow seas.

The Rochefort squadron duly escaped; Villeneuve, too, in command of the Toulon squadron, aided by the weather, evaded Nelson's watchfulness and disappeared towards the east. Nelson, however, suspected the real plan, and with fine insight took up a position which must have intercepted Villeneuve; but that admiral found the weather too rough for his ships, and ran back into Toulon. "These gentlemen," said Nelson, "are not accustomed to a Gulf of Lyons gale. We have faced them for twenty-one months, and not lost a spar!" The Rochefort squadron was, of course, left by its own success wandering in space, a mere cluster of sea-vagrants.

By March 1805, Napoleon had a new combination prepared. In the ports between Brest and Toulon were scattered no less than sixty-seven French or Spanish ships of the line. Ganteaume, with his squadron, was to break out from Brest; Villeneuve, with his, from Toulon; both fleets were to rendezvous at Martinique, return by an unusual route, and appear off Boulogne, a great fleet of thirty-five French ships of the line.

About the end of June the Toulon fleet got safely out—Nelson being, for once, badly served by his frigates—picked up additional ships off Cadiz, and disappeared on its route to the West Indies. Nelson, misled by false intelligence, first went eastward, then had to claw back through the Straits of Gibraltar in the teeth of strong westerly gales, and plunged over the horizon in fierce pursuit of Villeneuve. But the watch kept by Cornwallis over Ganteaume in Brest was so close and stern that escape was impossible, and one-half of Napoleon's combination broke down. Napoleon despatched swift ships on Villeneuve's track, summoning him back to Ferrol, where he would find a squadron of fifteen French and Spanish ships ready to join him. Villeneuve, Napoleon believed, had thoroughly deceived Nelson. "Those boasted English," he wrote, "who claim to know of everything, know nothing of it," *i.e.* of Villeneuve's escape and course. But the "boasted English," as a matter of fact, did know all about it, and in place of weakening their forces in the Bay of Biscay, strengthened them. Meanwhile Nelson, with ten ships of the line, was hard on the track of Villeneuve with eighteen. At Barbadoes, Nelson was sent a hundred miles out of his course by false intelligence, and that hundred miles just enabled Villeneuve to double back towards Europe.

Nelson divined this plan, and followed him with the fiercest energy, sending off, meanwhile, his fastest brig to warn the Admiralty. Villeneuve, if he picked up the Ferrol and Rochefort squadrons, would arrive off Brest with forty line-of-battle ships; if he raised the blockade, and added Ganteaume's squadron to his own, he might appear off Boulogne with sixty great ships! Napoleon calculated on British blunders to aid him. "We have not to do with a far-sighted, but with a very proud Government," he wrote. The blunder Napoleon hoped the British Admiralty would make was that of weakening the blockading squadrons in order to pursue Villeneuve's fleet, and thus release the imprisoned French squadrons, making a great concentration possible.

But this was exactly the blunder into which the Admiralty refused to be tempted. When the news that Villeneuve was on his way back to Europe reached the Admiralty, the First Lord, Barham, an old sailor, eighty years of age, without waiting to dress himself, dictated orders which, without weakening the blockades at any vital point, planted a fleet, under Sir Robert Calder, west of Finisterre, and right in Villeneuve's track; and if Calder had been Nelson, Trafalgar might have been fought on July 22, instead of October 21. Calder fought, and captured two of Villeneuve's ships, but failed to prevent the junction of Villeneuve's fleet with the squadron in Ferrol, and was court-martialled for his failure—victory though he called it. But this partial failure does not make less splendid the promptitude shown by the British Admiralty. "The English Admiralty," Napoleon reasoned, "could not decide the movements of its squadron in twenty-four hours." As a matter of fact, Barham decided the British strategy in almost as many minutes!

Meanwhile Nelson had reached the scene; and, like his ship, worn out with labours, sailed for Portsmouth, for what proved his last visit to England. On August 13, Villeneuve sailed from Ferrol with twenty-nine ships. He had his choice between Brest, where Cornwallis was keeping guard, with Boulogne beyond, and where Napoleon was watching eagerly for the white topsails of his fleet; or Cadiz, where Collingwood with a tiny squadron held the Spanish fleet strictly bottled up.

Villeneuve's true course was Boulogne, but Cornwallis lay in his path with over thirty sail of the line, and Villeneuve's nerve failed him. On August 21 he swung round and bore up for Cadiz; and with the turn of the helm which swung Villeneuve's ship away from Boulogne, Napoleon's last chance of invading England vanished. Villeneuve pushed Collingwood's tiny squadron aside and entered Cadiz, where the combined fleet now numbered nearly forty ships of the line, and Collingwood, with delightful coolness, solemnly resumed his blockade—four ships, that is, blockading forty! Napoleon gave way to a tempest of rage when his fleet failed to appear off Boulogne, and he realised that the British sailors he despised had finally thwarted his strategy. A French writer has told how Daru, his secretary, found him walking up and down his cabinet with agitated steps. With a voice that shook, and in half-strangled exclamations, he cried, "What a navy! What sacrifices for nothing! What an admiral! All hope is gone! That Villeneuve, instead of entering the Channel, has taken refuge in Ferrol. It is all over. He will be blockaded there." Then with that swift and terrible power of decision in which he has never been surpassed, he flung the long-cherished plan of invading England out of his brain, and dictated the orders which launched his troops on the road which led to Austerlitz and Jena, and, beyond, to the flames of Moscow and the snows of the great retreat, and which finally led Napoleon himself to

St. Helena. Villeneuve's great fleet meanwhile lay idle in Cadiz, till, on October 20, the ill-fated French admiral led his ships out to meet Nelson in his last great sea-fight.

II. HOW THE FLEETS MET

It was the night of October 20, 1805, a night moonless and black. In the narrow waters at the western throat of the Straits of Gibraltar, at regular intervals of three minutes through the whole night, the deep voice of a gun broke out and swept, a pulse of dying sound, almost to either coast, while at every half-hour a rocket soared aloft and broke in a curve of stars in the black sky. It was one of Nelson's re-peating frigates signalling to the British fleet, far off to the south-west, Villeneuve's movements. Nelson for more than a week had been trying to daintily coax Villeneuve out of Cadiz, as an angler might try to coax a much-experienced trout from the cool depths of some deep pool. He kept the main body of his fleet sixty leagues distant—west of Cape St. Mary—but kept a chain of frigates within signalling dis-tance of each other betwixt Cadiz and himself. He allowed the news that he had detached five of his line-of-battle ships on convoy duty to the eastward to leak through to the French admiral, but succeeded in keeping him in ignorance of the fact that he had called in under his flag five ships of equal force from the westward.

On October 19, Villeneuve, partly driven by hunger, and by the news that a successor was on the road from Paris to displace him, and partly tempted by the belief that he had before him a British fleet of only twenty-one ships of the line, crept out of Cadiz with thirty-three ships of the line—of which three were three-deckers—and seven frig-ates. Nelson had twenty-seven sail of the line with four frigates. The wind was light, and all through the 20th, Villeneuve's fleet, formed in seven columns—the *Santissima Trinidad* towering like a giant amongst them—moved slowly eastward. Nelson would not alarm his foe by making too early an appearance over the sky-line. His frigates signalled to him every few minutes, through sixty miles of sea-air, the enemy's movements; but Nelson himself held aloof till Villeneuve was too far from Cadiz to make a dash back to it and safety. All through the night of the 20th, Villeneuve's great fleet—a procession of mighty phantoms—was dimly visible against the Spanish coast, and the British frigates sent the news in alternate pulses of sound and flame to Nelson, by this time eagerly bearing up from Cape St. Mary.

The morning of the 21st broke misty, yet bright. The sea was almost like a floor of glass. The faintest of sea-airs blew. A lazy Atlantic swell rolled at long intervals towards the Straits, and the two fleets at last were visible to each other. Villeneuve's ships stretched a waving and slightly curved line, running north and south, with no regularity of order. The British fleet, in two compact and parallel columns, half a mile apart, came majestically on from the west. The ships in each column followed each other so closely that sometimes the bow of one was thrust past the quarter of the ship in advance of it. Nelson, in the *Victory*, headed one column, Collingwood, in the *Royal Sovereign*, led the other, and each flagship, it was to be noted, led with a clear interval between itself and its supports.

Villeneuve had a tactician's brain, and his battle-plan was admirable. In a general order, issued just before leading out his fleet, he told his captains, "There is nothing to alarm us in the sight of an English fleet. Their 64-gun ships have not 500 men on board; they are not more brave than we are;

they are harassed by a two-years' cruise; they have fewer motives to fight well!" Villeneuve explained that the enemy would attack in column, the French would meet the attack in close line of battle; and, with a touch of Nelson's spirit, he urged his captains to take every opportunity of boarding, and warned them that every ship not under fire would be counted a defaulter.

Nelson's plan was simple and daring. The order of sailing was to be the order of battle. Collingwood leading one column, and he the other, would pierce the enemy's lines at points which would leave some twelve of the enemy's ships to be crushed betwixt the two British lines. Nelson, whose brooding genius forecast every changing eddy of battle, gave minute instructions on a score of details. To prevent mistakes amid the smoke and the fight, for example, he had the hoops on the masts of every British ship painted yellow; every ship was directed to fly a St. George's ensign, with the Union Jack at the fore-topmast, and another flying from the top-gallant stays. That he would beat the enemy's fleet he calmly took for granted, but he directed that every effort should be made to capture its commander-in-chief. Nelson crowned his instructions with the characteristic remark, that "in case signals were obscure, no captain can do wrong if he places his ship alongside of an enemy."

By twelve o'clock the two huge fleets were slowly approaching each other: the British columns compact, grim, orderly; the Franco-Spanish line loose, but magnificently picturesque, a far-stretching line of lofty hulls, a swaying forest of sky-piercing masts. They still preserve the remark of one prosaic British sailor, who, surveying the enemy through an open port, offered the comment, "What a fine sight, Bill, yon ships would make at Spithead!"

It is curious to reflect how exactly both British and French invert on sea their land tactics. French infantry attack in column, and are met by British infantry in line; and the line, with its steadfast courage and wide front of fire, crushes the column. On sea, on the other hand, the British attack in column, and the French meet the attack in line; but the column wins. But it must be admitted that the peril of this method of attack is enormous. The leading ship approaches, stern on, to a line of fire which, if steady enough, may well crush her by its concentration of flame. Attack in column, in fact, means that the leading ships are sacrificed to secure victory for the ships in the rear. The risks of this method of attack at Trafalgar were enormously increased by the light and uncertain quality of the wind. Collingwood, in the *Royal Sovereign*, and Nelson, in the *Victory*, as a matter of fact, drifted slowly rather than sailed, stern on to the broadsides of their enemy. The leading British ships, with their stately heights of swelling canvas, moved into the raking fire of the far-stretching Franco-Spanish line at a speed of about two knots an hour. His officers knew that Nelson's ship, carrying the flag of the commander-in-chief, as it came slowly on, would be the mark for every French gunner, and must pass through a tempest of flame before it could fire a shot in reply; and Blackwood begged Nelson to let the *Téméraire*—"the fighting *Téméraire*"—take the *Victory's* place at the head of the column. "Oh yes, let her go ahead," answered Nelson, with a queer smile; and the *Téméraire* was hailed, and ordered to take the lead. But Nelson meant that the *Téméraire* should take the *Victory's* place only if she could, and he watched grimly to see that not a sheet was let fly or a sail shortened to give the *Téméraire* a chance of passing; and so the *Victory* kept its proud and perilous lead.

Collingwood led the lee division, and had the honour of beginning the mighty drama of Trafalgar. The *Royal Sovereign* was newly coppered, and, with every inch of canvas outspread, got so far ahead of her followers, that after Collingwood had broken into the French line, he sustained its fire, unhelped, for nearly twenty minutes before the *Belleisle*, the ship next following, could fire a gun for his help.

Of Collingwood, Thackeray says, "I think, since Heaven made gentlemen, it never made a better one than Cuthbert Collingwood," and there was, no doubt, a knightly and chivalrous side to Collingwood worthy of King Arthur's round table. But there was also a side of heavy-footed common-sense, of Dutch-like frugality, in Collingwood, a sort of wooden-headed unimaginativeness which looks humorous when set against the background of such a planet-shaking fight as Trafalgar. Thus on the morning of the fight he advised one of his lieutenants, who wore a pair of boots, to follow his example and put on stockings and shoes, as, in the event of being shot in the leg, it would, he explained, "be so much more manageable for the surgeon." And as he walked the break of his poop in tights, silk stockings, and buckled shoes, leading, in his single ship, an attack on a fleet, he calmly munched an apple. To be able to munch an apple when beginning Trafalgar is an illustration of what may be called the quality of wooden-headed unimaginativeness in Collingwood. And yet Collingwood had a sense of the scale of the drama in which he was taking part. "Now, gentlemen," he said to his officers, "let us do something to-day which the world may talk of hereafter." Collingwood, in reality, was a great man and a great seaman, and in the battle which followed he "fought like an angel," to quote the amusingly inappropriate metaphor of Blackwood.

The two majestic British columns moved slowly on, the great ships, with ports hauled up and guns run out, following each other like a procession of giants. "I suppose," says Codrington, who commanded the *Orion*, "no man ever before saw such a sight." And the element of humour was added to the scene by the spectacle of the tiny *Pickle*, a duodecimo schooner, gravely hanging on to the quarter of an 80-gun ship—as an actor in the fight describes it—"with the boarding-nettings up, and her tompions out of her four guns—about as large and as formidable as two pairs of Wellington boots."

Collingwood bore down to the fight a clear quarter of a mile ahead of the next ship. The fire of the enemy, like so many spokes of flame converging to a centre, broke upon him. But in silence the great ship moved ahead to a gap in the line between the *Santa Anna*, a huge black hulk of 112 guns, and the *Neptune*, of 74. As the bowsprit of the *Royal Sovereign* slowly glided past the stern of the *Santa Anna*, Collingwood, as Nelson had ordered all his captains, cut his studding-sails loose, and they fell, a cloud of white canvas, into the water. Then as the broadside of the *Royal Sovereign* fairly covered the stern of the *Santa Anna*, Collingwood spoke. He poured with deadly aim and suddenness, and at pistol-shot distance, his whole broadside into the Spaniard's stern. The tempest of shot swept the unhappy *Santa Anna* from end to end, and practically destroyed that vessel. Some 400 of its crew are said to have been killed or wounded by that single discharge! At the same moment Collingwood discharged his other broadside at the *Neptune*, though with less effect; then swinging round broadside to broadside on the Spanish ship, he swept its decks again and again with his guns. The first broadside had practically done the Spaniard's business; but its captain, a gallant man, still returned what fire he could. All the enemy's ships within reach of Collingwood had meanwhile opened on him a dreadful fire; no fewer than five line-of-battle ships were emptying their guns upon the *Royal Sovereign* at one time, and it seemed marvellous that the British ship was not shattered to mere splinters by the fire poured from so many quarters upon her. It was like being in the heart of a volcano. Frequently, it is said, the British saw the flying cannon-balls meet in mid-air. The seamen fell fast, the sails were torn, the bulwarks shattered, the decks ran red with blood. It was at that precise moment, however, that Collingwood said to his captain, "What would not Nelson give to be here!" While at the same instant Nelson was saying to Hardy, "See how that noble fellow Collingwood takes his ship into action!"

The other ships of Collingwood's column were by this time slowly drifting into the fight. At a quarter past twelve the *Belleisle*, the next ship, ranged under the stern of the unfortunate *Santa Anna*, and fired her larboard guns, double shotted, into that ship, with the result that her three masts fell over the side. She then steered for the *Indomptable*, an 80-gun ship, and sustained at the same moment the fire of two Spanish seventy-fours. Ship after ship of Collingwood's column came steadily up, and the roar of the battle deepened as in quick-following crashes each new line-of-battle ship broke into the thunder of broadsides.

Nelson, leading the weather column, steered a trifle to the northward, as the slowly moving line of the enemy pointed towards Cadiz. Nelson had given his last orders. At his mainmast head was flying, fast belayed, the signal, "Engage the enemy more closely." Nelson himself walked

quietly to and fro on the little patch of clear plank, scarcely seven yards long, on the quarter-deck of the *Victory*, whence he could command the whole ship, and he wore the familiar threadbare frock uniform coat, bearing on the left breast four tarnished and lack-lustre stars. Then came the incident of the immortal signal. "We must give the fleet," said Nelson to Blackwood, "something by way of a fillip." After musing a while, he said, "Suppose we signal, 'Nelson confides that every man will do his duty'?" Some one suggested "England" instead of "Nelson," and Nelson at once caught at the improvement. The signal-officer explained that the word "confide" would have to be spelt, and suggested instead the word "expects," as that was in the vocabulary. So the flags on the masthead of the *Victory* spelt out the historic sentence to the slowly moving fleet. That the signal was "received with cheers" is scarcely accurate. The message was duly acknowledged, and recorded in the log of every ship, but perhaps not one man in every hundred of the actors at Trafalgar knew at the moment that it had been sent. But the message rings in British ears yet, across ninety years, and will ring in the ears of generations yet unborn.

Nelson led his column on a somewhat slanting course into the fight. He was bent on laying himself alongside the flagship of the enemy, and he knew that this must be one of the three great line-of-battle ships near the huge *Santissima Trinidad*. But there was no sign to show which of the three carried Villeneuve. At half-past twelve the ships upon which the *Victory* was moving began to fire single shots at her slowly drifting hulk to discover whether she was within range. The seventh of these shots, fired at intervals of a minute or so, tore a rent through the upper canvas of the

Victory—a rent still to be seen in the carefully preserved sail. A couple of minutes of awful silence followed. Slowly the *Victory* drifted on its path, and then no fewer than eight of the great ships upon which the *Victory* was moving broke into such a tempest of shot as perhaps never before was poured on a single ship. One of the first shots killed Scott, Nelson's secretary; another cut down eight marines standing in line on the *Victory's* quarter-deck; a third passed between Nelson and Hardy as they stood side by side. "Too warm work to last long, Hardy," said Nelson, with a smile. Still the *Victory* drifted majestically on its fiery path without an answering gun.

The French line was irregular at this point, the ships lying, in some instances, two or three deep, and this made the business of "cutting" the line difficult. As Nelson could not pick out the French flagship, he said to Hardy, "Take your choice, go on board which you please;" and Hardy pointed the stern of the Victory towards a gap between the *Redoutable*, a 74-gun ship, and the *Bucentaure*. But the ship moved slowly. The fire upon it was tremendous. One shot drove a shower of splinters upon both Nelson and Hardy; nearly fifty men and officers had been killed or wounded; the *Victory's* sails were riddled, her studding-sail booms shot off close to the yard-arm, her mizzen-topmast, shot away. At one o'clock, however, the *Victory* slowly moved past the stern of the *Bucentaure*, and a 68-pounder carronade on its forecastle, charged with a round shot and a keg of 500 musket balls, was fired into the cabin windows of the French ship. Then, as the great ship moved on, every gun of the remaining fifty that formed its broadside—some of them double and treble loaded—was fired through the Frenchman's cabin windows.

The dust from the crumpled woodwork of the *Bucentaure's* stern covered the persons of Nelson and the group of officers standing on the *Victory's* quarter-deck, while the British sailors welcomed with a fierce shout the crash their flying shot made within the Frenchman's hull. The *Bucentaure*, as it happened—though Nelson was ignorant of the fact—was the French flagship; and after the battle its officers declared that by this single broadside, out of its crew of nearly 1000 men, nearly 400 were struck down, and no less than twenty guns dismounted!

But the *Neptune*, a fine French 80-gun ship, lay right across the water-lane up which the *Victory* was moving, and it poured upon the British ship two raking broadsides of the most deadly quality. The *Victory*, however, moved on unflinchingly, and the *Neptune*, fearing to be run aboard by the British ship, set her jib and moved ahead; then the *Victory* swung to starboard on to the *Redoutable*. The French ship fired one hurried broadside, and promptly shut her lower-deck ports, fearing the British sailors would board through them. No fewer, indeed, than five French line-of-battle ships during the fight, finding themselves grinding sides with British ships, adopted the same course—an expressive testimony to the enterprising quality of British sailors. The *Victory*, however, with her lower-deck guns actually touching the side of the *Redoutable*, still kept them in full and quick action; but at each of the lower-deck ports stood a sailor with a bucket of water, and when the gun was fired—its muzzle touching the wooden sides of the *Redoutable*—the water was dashed upon the ragged hole made by the shot, to prevent the Frenchman taking fire and both ships being consumed.

The guns on the upper deck of the *Victory* speedily

swept and silenced the upper deck of the *Redoutable*, and as far as its broadsides were concerned, that ship was helpless. Its tops, however, were crowded with marksmen, and armed with brass coehorns, firing langrage shot, and these scourged with a pitiless and most deadly fire the decks of the *Victory*, while the *Bucentaure* and the gigantic *Santissima Trinidad* also thundered on the British flagship.

III. How the Victory Was Won

Nelson's strategy at Trafalgar is described quaintly, but with real insight, in a sentence which a Spanish novelist, Don Perez Galdos, puts into the mouth of one of his characters: "Nelson, who, as everybody knows, was no fool, saw our long line and said, 'Ah, if I break through that in two places, and put the part of it between the two places between two fires, I shall grab every stick of it.' That was exactly what the confounded fellow did. And as our line was so long that the head couldn't help the tail, he worried us from end to end, while he drove his two wedges into our body." It followed that the flaming vortex of the fight was in that brief mile of sea-space, between the two points where the parallel British lines broke through Villeneuve's swaying forest of masts. And the tempest of sound and flame was fiercest, of course, round the two ships that carried the flags of Nelson and Collingwood. As each stately British liner, however, drifted—rather than sailed—into the black pall of smoke, the roar of the fight deepened and widened until the whole space between the *Royal Sovereign* and the *Victory* was shaken with mighty pulse-beats of sound that marked the furious and quick-following broadsides.

The scene immediately about the *Victory* was very remarkable. The *Victory* had run foul of the *Redoutable*, the anchors of the two ships hooking into each other. The concussion of the broadsides would, no doubt, have driven the two hulls apart, but that the *Victory's* studding-sail boom iron had fastened, like a claw, into the leech of the Frenchman's fore-topsail. The *Téméraire*, coming majestically up through the smoke, raked the *Bucentaure*, and closed with a crash on the starboard side of the *Redoutable*, and the four great ships lay in a solid tier, while between their huge grinding sides came, with a sound and a glare almost resembling the blast of an exploding mine, the flash, the smoke, the roar of broadside after broadside.

In the whole heroic fight there is no finer bit of heroism than that shown by the *Redoutable*. She was only a 74-gun ship, and she had the *Victory*, of 100 guns, and the *Téméraire*, of 98, on either side. It is true these ships had to fight at the same time with a whole ring of antagonists; nevertheless, the fire poured on the *Redoutable* was so fierce that only courage of a steel-like edge and temper could have sustained it. The gallant French ship was semi-dismasted, her hull shot through in every direction, one-fourth of her guns were dismounted. Out of a crew of 643, no fewer than 523 were killed or wounded. Only 35, indeed, lived to reach England as prisoners. And yet she fought on. The fire from her great guns, indeed, soon ceased, but the deadly splutter of musketry from such of her tops as were yet standing was maintained; and, as Brenton put it, "there was witnessed for nearly an hour and a half the singular spectacle of a French 74-gun ship engaging a British first and second rate, with small-arms only."

As a matter of fact, the *Victory* repeatedly ceased firing, believing that the *Redoutable* had struck, but still the venomous and deadly fire from the tops of that vessel continued;

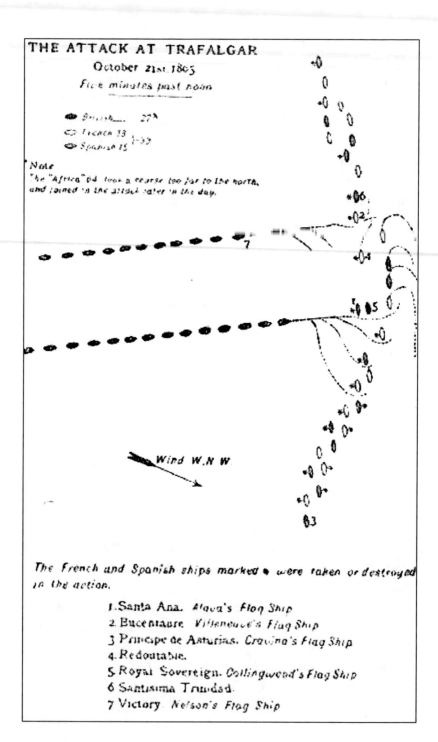

THE ATTACK AT TRAFALGAR

October 21st 1805

Five minutes past noon

British — 27
French 18
Spanish 15 } 33

Note
The "Africa" had took a course too far to the north,
and joined in the attack later in the day.

7

Wind W.N.W

The French and Spanish ships marked * were taken or destroyed
in the action.

1. Santa Ana. Alava's Flag Ship
2. Bucentaure. Villeneuve's Flag Ship
3. Principe de Asturias. Gravina's Flag Ship
4. Redoutable.
5. Royal Sovereign. Collingwood's Flag Ship
6. Santisima Trinidad.
7. Victory. Nelson's Flag Ship

and it was to this circumstance, indeed, that Nelson owed his death. He would never put small-arms men in his own tops, as he believed their fire interfered with the working of the sails, and, indeed, ran the risk of igniting them. Thus the French marksmen that crowded the tops of the *Redoutable* had it all their own way; and as the distance was short, and their aim deadly, nearly every man on the poop, quarter-deck, and forecastle of the *Victory* was shot down.

Nelson, with Hardy by his side, was walking backwards and forwards on a little clear space of the *Victory's* quarter-deck, when he suddenly swung round and fell face down-wards on the deck. Hardy picked him up. "They have done for me at last, Hardy," said Nelson; "my backbone is shot through." A musket bullet from the *Redoutable's* mizzen-top—only fifteen yards distant—had passed through the forepart of the epaulette, smashed a path through the left shoulder, and lodged in the spine. The evidence seems to make it clear that it was a chance shot that wrought the fatal mischief. Hardy had twice the bulk of Nelson's in-significant figure, and wore a more striking uniform, and would certainly have attracted the aim of a marksman in preference to Nelson.

Few stories are more pathetic or more familiar than that of Nelson's last moments. As they carried the dying hero across the blood-splashed decks, and down the ladders into the cock-pit, he drew a handkerchief over his own face and over the stars on his breast, lest the knowledge that he was struck down should discourage his crew. He was stripped, his wound probed, and it was at once known to be mortal. Nelson suffered greatly; he was consumed with thirst, had to be fanned with sheets of paper; and he kept constantly pushing away the sheet, the sole covering over him, saying,

"Fan, fan," or "Drink, drink," and one attendant was constantly employed in drawing the sheet over his thin limbs and emaciated body. Presently Hardy, snatching a moment from the fight raging on the deck, came to his side, and the two comrades clasped hands. "Well, Hardy, how goes the battle?" Nelson asked. He was told that twelve or fourteen of the enemy's ships had struck. "That is well," said Nelson, "but I had bargained for twenty." Then his seaman's brain forecasting the change of weather, and picturing the battered ships with their prizes on a lee shore, he exclaimed emphatically, "Anchor! Hardy, anchor!" Hardy hinted that Collingwood would take charge of affairs. "Not while I live, I hope, Hardy," said the dying chief, trying to raise himself on his bed. "No! do you anchor, Hardy."

Many of Nelson's expressions, recorded by his doctor, Beatty, are strangely touching. "I am a dead man, Hardy," he said, "I am going fast. It will all be over with me soon." "O *Victory, Victory*," he said, as the great ship shook to the roar of her own guns, "how you distract my poor brain!" "How dear is life to all men!" he said, after a pause. He begged that "his carcass might be sent to England, and not thrown overboard." So in the dim cock-pit, with the roar of the great battle—bellow of gun, and shout of cheering crews—filling all the space about him, and his last thoughts yet busy for his country, the soul of the greatest British seaman passed away. "Kiss me, Hardy," was one of his last sentences. His last intelligible sentence was, "I have done my duty; I praise God for it."

It may interest many to read the prayer which Nelson wrote—the last record, but one, he made in his diary—and written as the final act of preparation for Trafalgar: "May the great God, whom I worship, grant to my country, and for the benefit of Europe in general, a great and glorious victory; and may no misconduct in any one tarnish it; and may humanity after victory be the predominant feature in the British fleet. For myself individually, I commit my life to Him that made me, and may His blessing alight on my endeavours for serving my country faithfully. To Him I resign myself, and the just cause which is entrusted to me to defend. Amen, Amen, Amen."

Nelson's plan allowed his captains a large discretion in the choice of their antagonists. Each British ship had to follow the wake of her leader till she reached the enemy's line, then her captain was free to choose his own foe—which, naturally, was the biggest Frenchman or Spaniard in sight. And the huge *Santissima Trinidad*, of course, attracted the eager attention of the ships that immediately followed the *Victory*. The Spaniard carried 140 guns, and in that swaying continent of fighting ships, towered like a giant amongst dwarfs. The *Neptune*, the *Leviathan*, and the *Conqueror*, in turn, hung on the quarter or broadside of the gigantic Spaniard, scourged it with fire, and then drifted off to engage in a fiery wrestle with some other antagonist. By half-past two the Spanish four-decker was a mastless wreck. The *Neptune* at that moment was hanging on her bow, the *Conqueror* on her quarter. "This tremendous fabric," says an account written by an officer on board the Conqueror, "gave a deep roll, with a swell to leeward, then back to windward, and on her return every mast went by the board, leaving her an unmanageable hulk on the water. Her immense topsails had every reef out, her royals were sheeted home but lowered, and the falling of this majestic mass of spars, sails, and rigging plunging into the water at the muzzles of our guns, was one of the most magnificent sights I ever beheld." Directly after this a Spaniard waved an English union over the lee gangway of the *Santissima Trinidad* in token of surrender; whereupon the *Conqueror*, scorning to waste time in taking possession of even a four-decker that had no longer any fight in it, pushed off in search of a new foe; while the *Neptune's* crew proceeded to shift the tattered topsails of their ship for new ones, with as much coolness as though in a friendly port.

The *Africa*, sixty-four, less than half the size of the Spaniard, presently came slowly up through the smoke, and fired into the Spanish ship; then seeing no flag flying, sent a lieutenant on board the mastless hulk to take possession. The Englishman climbed to the quarterdeck, all black with smoke and bloody with slaughter, and asked the solitary officer he found there whether or not the *Santissima Trinidad* had surrendered. The ship, as a matter of fact, was drifting into the centre of a cluster of French and Spanish ships; so the Spaniard replied, "Non, non," at the same time pointing to the friendly ships upon which they were drifting. The Englishman had only half-a-dozen men with him, so he coolly returned to his boat, and the *Santissima Trinidad* drifted like a log upon the water till half-past five P.M., when the *Prince* put a prize crew on board.

Perez Galdos has given a realistic picture—quoted in the *Cornhill Magazine*—of the scenes within the gloomy recesses of the great Spanish four-decker as the British ships hung on her flanks and wasted her with their fire: "The English shot had torn our sails to tatters. It was as if huge invisible talons had been dragging at them. Fragments of spars, splinters of wood, thick hempen cables cut up as corn is cut by the sickle, fallen blocks, shreds of canvas, bits of iron, and hundreds of other things that had been wrenched away by the enemy's fire, were piled along the deck, where it was scarcely possible to move about. From moment to moment men fell—some into the sea; and the curses of the combatants mingled with groans of the wounded, so that it was often difficult to decide whether the dying were blaspheming God or the fighters were calling upon Him for aid. I helped in the very dismal task of carrying the wounded into the hold, where the surgeons worked. Some died ere we could convey them thither; others had to undergo frightful operations ere their worn-out bodies could get an instant's rest. It was much more satisfactory to be able to assist the carpenter's crew in temporarily stopping some of the holes torn by shot in the ship's hull. . . . Blood ran in streams about the deck; and, in spite of the sand, the rolling of the ship carried it hither and thither until it made strange patterns on the planks. The enemy's shot, fired, as they were, from very short range, caused horrible mutilations. . . . The ship creaked and groaned as she rolled, and through a thousand holes and crevices in her strained hull the sea spurted in and began to flood the hold. The *Trinidad's* people saw the commander-in-chief haul down his flag; heard the *Achille* blow up and hurl her six hundred men into eternity; learnt that their own hold was so crowded with wounded that no more could be received there. Then, when all three masts had in succession been brought crashing down, the defence collapsed, and the *Santissima Trinidad* struck her flag."

The dreadful scenes on the decks of the *Santissima Trinidad* might almost have been paralleled on some of the British ships. Thus the *Belleisle*, Collingwood's immediate supporter, sustained the fire of two French and one Spanish line-of-battle ships until she was dismasted. The wreck of her mizzen-mast covered her larboard guns, her mainmast fell upon the break of the poop; her larboard broadside was thus rendered useless; and just then another French line-of-battle ship, the *Achille*, took her position on the *Belleisle's* larboard quarter, and opened on her a deadly fire, to which the British ship could not return a shot. This scene lasted for nearly an hour and a half, but at half past three the *Swiftsure* came majestically up, passed under the *Belleisle's* stern—the two crews cheering each other, the *Belleisle's* men waving a Union Jack at the end of a pike to show they were still fighting, while an ensign still flew from the stump of the mainmast—and the fury with which the *Swiftsure* fell upon the *Achille* may be imagined. The *Defiance* about the same time took off the *Aigle*, and the *Polyphemus* the *Neptune*, and the much-battered *Belleisle* floated free. Masts, bowsprit, boats, figurehead—all were shot away; her hull was pierced in every direction; she was a mere splintered wreck.

The *Téméraire* fought a battle almost as dreadful. The *Africa*, a light ship carrying only sixty-four guns, chose as her antagonist the *Intrépide*, a French seventy-four, in weight of broadside and number of crew almost double her force. How dreadful were the damages sustained by the British ship in a fight so unequal and so stubborn may be imagined; but she clung to her big antagonist until, the *Orion* coming up, the *Intrépide* struck.

At three P.M. the firing had begun to slacken, and ship after ship of the enemy was striking. At a quarter past two the *Algeziras* struck to the *Tonnant*, and fifteen minutes afterwards the *San Juan*—the *Tonnant* was fighting both ships—also hailed that she surrendered. Lieutenant Clement was sent in the jolly-boat, with two hands, to take possession of the Spanish seventy-four, and the boat carrying the gallant three was struck by a shot and swamped. The sailors could swim, but not the lieutenant; the pair of tars succeeded in struggling back with their officer to the *Tonnant*; and as that ship had not another boat that would float, she had to see her prize drift off. The *Colossus*, in like manner, fought with the French *Swiftsure* and the *Bahama*—each her own size—and captured them both! The *Redoutable* had surrendered by this time, and a couple of midshipmen, with a dozen hands, had climbed from the *Victory's* one remaining boat through the stern ports of the French ship. The *Bucentaure*, Villeneuve's flagship, had her fate practically sealed by the first tremendous broadside poured into her by the *Victory*. With fine courage, however, the French ship maintained a straggling fire until both the *Leviathan* and the *Conqueror*, at a distance of less than thirty yards, were pouring a tempest of shot into her. The French flagship then struck, and was taken possession of by a tiny boat's crew from the *Conqueror* consisting of three marines and two sailors. The marine officer coolly locked the powder magazine of the Frenchman, put the key in his pocket, left two of his men in charge of the surrendered *Bucentaure*, put Villeneuve and his two captains in his boat with his two marines and himself, and went off in search of the *Conqueror*. In the smoke and confusion, however, he could not find that ship, and so carried the captured French admiral to the *Mars*. Hercules Robinson has drawn a pen picture of the unfortunate French admiral as he came on board the British ship: "Villeneuve was a tallish, thin man, a very tranquil, placid, English-looking Frenchman; he wore a long-tailed uniform coat, high and flat collar, corduroy pantaloons of a greenish colour with stripes two inches wide, half-boots with sharp toes, and a watch-chain with long gold links. Majendie was a short, fat, jocund sailor, who found a cure for all ills in the Frenchman's philosophy, *"Fortune de la guerre"* (though this was the third time the goddess had brought him to England as a prisoner); and he used to tell our officers very tough stories of the 'Mysteries of Paris.'"

By five o'clock the roar of guns had died almost into silence. Of thirty-three stately battle-ships that formed the Franco-Spanish fleet four hours earlier, one had vanished in flames, seventeen were captured as mere blood-stained hulks, and fifteen were in flight; while Villeneuve himself was a prisoner. But Nelson was dead. Night was falling. A fierce south-east gale was blowing. A sea—such a sea as only arises in shallow waters—ugly, broken, hollow, was rising fast. In all directions ships dismantled, with scuppers crimson with blood, and sides jagged with shot-holes, were rolling their tall, huge hulks in the heavy sea; and the shoals of Trafalgar were only thirteen miles to leeward! The fight with tempest and sea during that terrific night was almost more dreadful than the battle with human foes during the day. Codrington says, the gale was so furious that "it blew away the top main-topsail, though it was close-reefed, and the fore-topsail after it was clewed up ready for furling." They dare not set a storm staysail, although now within six miles of the reef. The *Redoutable* sank at the stern of the ship towing it; the *Bucentaure* had to be cut adrift, and went to pieces on the shoals. The wind shifted in the night and enabled the shot-wrecked and storm-battered ships to claw off the shore; but the fierce weather still raged, and on the 24th the huge *Santissima Trinidad* had to be cut adrift. It was night; wind and sea were furious; but the boats of the *Ajax* and the *Nep-*

tune succeeded in rescuing every wounded man on board the huge Spaniard. The boats, indeed, had all put off when a cat ran out on the muzzle of one of the lower-deck guns and mewed plaintively, and one of the boats pulled back, in the teeth of wind and sea, and rescued poor puss!

Of the eighteen British prizes, fourteen sank, were wrecked, burnt by the captors, or recaptured; only four reached Portsmouth. Yet never was the destruction of a fleet more absolutely complete. Of the fifteen ships that escaped Trafalgar, four were met in the open sea on November 4 by an equal number of British ships, under Sir Richard Strahan, and were captured. The other eleven lay disabled hulks in Cadiz till—when France and Spain broke into war with each other—they were all destroyed. Villeneuve's great fleet, in brief, simply vanished from existence! But Napoleon, with that courageous economy of truth characteristic of him, summed up Trafalgar in the sentence: "The storms occasioned to us the loss of a few ships after a battle imprudently fought"! Trafalgar, as a matter of fact, was the most amazing victory won by land or sea through the whole Revolutionary war. It permanently changed the course of history; and it goes far to justify Nelson's magnificently audacious boast, "The fleets of England are equal to meet the world in arms!"

CHAPTER 8

The Fire-Ships in the
Basque Roads

On the night of April 11, 1809, Lord Cochrane steered his floating mine against the gigantic boom that covered the French fleet lying in Aix Roads. The story is one of the most picturesque and exciting in the naval annals of Great Britain. Marryat has embalmed the great adventure and its chief actor in the pages of "Frank Mildmay," and Lord Cochrane himself—like the Earl of Peterborough in the seventeenth century, who captured Barcelona with a handful of men, and Gordon in the nineteenth century, who won great battles in China walking-stick in hand—was a man who stamped himself, as with characters of fire, upon the popular imagination.

To the courage of a knight-errant Cochrane added the shrewd and humorous sagacity of a Scotchman. If he had commanded fleets he would have rivalled the victories of Nelson, and perhaps even have outshone the Nile and Trafalgar. And to warlike genius of the first order Cochrane added a certain weird and impish ingenuity which his enemies found simply resistless. Was there ever a cruise in naval history like that of Cochrane in his brig misnamed the *Speedy*, a mere coasting tub that would neither steer nor tack, and whose entire broadside Cochrane himself could carry in his pockets! But in this wretched little brig, with its four-pounders, Cochrane captured in one brief year more than 50 vessels carrying an aggregate of 122 guns, took 500 prisoners, kept the whole Spanish coast, off which he cruised, in perpetual alarm, and finished by attacking and capturing a Spanish frigate, the *Gamo*, of 32 heavy guns and 319 men. What we have called the impish daring and resource of Cochrane is shown in this strange fight. He ran the little *Speedy* close under the guns of the huge *Gamo*, and the Spanish ship was actually unable to depress its guns sufficiently to harm its tiny antagonist. When the Spaniards tried to board, Cochrane simply shoved his pigmy craft a few yards away from the side of his foe, and this curious fight went on for an hour. Then, in his turn, Cochrane boarded, leaving nobody but the doctor on board the Speedy. But he played the Spaniards a characteristic trick. One half his men boarded the *Gamo* by the head, with their faces elaborately blackened; and when, out of the white smoke forward, some forty demons with black faces broke upon the astonished Spaniards, they naturally regarded the whole business as partaking of the black art, and incontinently fled below! The number of Spaniards killed and wounded in this fight by the little *Speedy* exceeded the number of its own entire crew; and when the fight was over, 45 British sailors had to keep guard over 263 Spanish prisoners.

Afterwards, in command of the *Impérieuse*, a fine frigate, Cochrane played a still more dashing part on the Spanish coast, destroying batteries, cutting off supplies from the French ports, blowing up coast roads, and keeping perspiring battalions of the enemy marching to and fro to meet his descents. On the French coast, again, Cochrane held large bodies of French troops paralysed by his single frigate. He proposed to the English Government to take possession of the French islands in the Bay of Biscay, and to allow him, with a small squadron of frigates, to operate against the French seaboard. Had this request been granted, he says, "neither the Peninsular war nor its enormous cost to the nation from 1809 onwards would ever have been heard of! It would have been easy," he adds, "as it always will be easy in case of future wars, so to harass the French coasts as to find full employment for their troops at home, and so to render operations in foreign countries impossible." If England and France were once more engaged in war—*absit omen!*—the story of Cochrane's exploits on the Spanish and French coasts might prove a very valuable inspiration and object-lesson. Cochrane's professional reward for his great services in the *Impérieuse* was an official rebuke for expending more sails, stores, gunpowder and shot than any other captain afloat in the same time!

The fight in the Basque Roads, however—or rather in the Aix Roads—has great historical importance. It crowned the work of Trafalgar. It finally destroyed French power on the sea, and gave England an absolute supremacy. No fleet actions took place after its date between "the meteor flag" and the tricolour, for the simple reason that no French fleet remained in existence. Cochrane's fire-ships completed the work of the Nile and Trafalgar.

Early in 1809 the French fleet in Brest, long blockaded by Lord Gambier, caught the British napping, slipped out unobserved, raised the blockades at L'Orient and Roche-fort, added the squadrons lying in these two places to its own strength, and, anchoring in the Aix Roads, prepared for a dash on the West Indies. The success with which the blockade at Brest had been evaded, and the menace offered to the West Indian trade, alarmed the British Admiralty. Lord Gambier, with a powerful fleet, kept guard outside the Aix Roads; but if the blockade failed once, it might fail again. Eager to destroy the last fleet France possessed, the Admiralty strongly urged Lord Gambier to attack the enemy with fire-ships; but Gambier, grown old, had visibly lost nerve, and he pronounced the use of fire-ships a "horrible and unchristian mode of warfare." Lord Mulgrave, the first Lord of the Admiralty, knowing Cochrane's ingenuity and daring, sent for him, and proposed to send him to the Basque Roads to invent and execute some plan for destroying the French fleet. The Scotchman was uppermost in Cochrane in this interview, and he declined the adventure on the ground that to send a young post-captain to execute such an enterprise would be regarded as an insult by the whole fleet, and he would have every man's hand against him. Lord Mulgrave, however, was peremptory, and Cochrane yielded, but on reaching the blockading fleet was met by a tempest of wrath from all his seniors. "Why," they asked, "was Cochrane sent out? We could have done the business as well as he. Why did not Lord Gambier let us do it?"

Lord Gambier, who had fallen into a sort of gentle and pious melancholy, was really more occupied in distributing tracts among his crews than in trying to reach his enemies; and Harvey, his second in command, an old Trafalgar sea-dog, when Cochrane arrived with his commission, interviewed his admiral, denounced him in a white-heat on his own quarter-deck, and ended by telling him that "if Nelson had been there he would not have anchored in the Basque Roads at all, but would have dashed at the enemy at once." This outburst, no doubt, relieved Admiral Harvey's feelings, but it cost him his flag, and he was court-martialled, and dismissed from the service for the performance.

Cochrane, however, set himself with characteristic daring and coolness to carry out his task. The French fleet consisted of one huge ship of 120 guns, two of 80 guns, eight seventy-fours, a 50-gun ship, and two 40-gun frigates—fourteen ships in all. It was drawn up in two lines under the shelter of powerful shore batteries, with the frigates as out-guards. As a protection against fire-ships, a gigantic boom had been constructed half a mile in length, forming two sides of a triangle, with the apex towards the British fleet. Over this huge floating barrier powerful boat squadrons kept watch every night. Cochrane's plan of attack was marked by real genius. He constructed three explosion vessels, floating mines on the largest scale. Each of these terrific vessels contained no less than *fifteen hundred* barrels of gunpowder, bound together with cables, with wedges and moistened sand rammed down betwixt them; forming, in brief, one gigantic bomb, with 1500 barrels of gunpowder for its charge. On the top of this huge powder magazine was piled, as a sort of agreeable condiment, hundreds of live shells and thousands of hand grenades; the whole, by every form of marine ingenuity, compacted into a solid mass which, at the touch of a fuse, could be turned into a sort of floating Vesuvius. These were to be followed by a squadron of fire-ships. Cochrane who, better, perhaps, than any soldier or sailor that ever lived, knew how to strike at his foes through their own imagination, calculated that when these three huge explosion vessels, with twenty fire-ships behind them, went off in a sort of saltpetre earthquake, the astonished Frenchmen would imagine *every* fire-ship to be a floating mine, and, instead of trying to board them and divert them from their fleet, would be simply anxious to get out of their way with the utmost possible despatch. The French, meanwhile, having watched their enemy lying inert for weeks, and confident in the gigantic boom which acted as their shield to the front, and the show of batteries which kept guard over them on either flank and to the rear, awaited the coming attack in a spirit of half-contemptuous gaiety. They had struck their topmasts and unbent their sails, and by way of challenge dressed their fleet with flags. One ship, the *Calcutta*, had been captured from the English, and by way of special insult they hung out the British ensign under that ship's quarter-gallery, an affront whose deadly quality only a sailor can understand.

The night of the 9th set in stormily. The tide ran fast, and the skies were black and the sea heavy—so heavy, indeed, that the boats of the English fleet which were intended to follow and cover the fire-ships never left the side of the flagship. Cochrane, however, had called the officers commanding the fire-ships on board his frigate, given them their last instructions, and at half-past eight P.M. he himself, accompanied only by a lieutenant and four sailors, cut the moorings of the chief explosion vessel, and drifted off towards the French fleet. Seated, that is, on top of 1500 barrels of gunpowder and a sort of haystack of grenades, he calmly floated off, with a squadron of fire-ships behind him, towards the French fleet, backed by great shore batteries, with seventy-three armed boats as a line of skirmishers. "It seemed to me," says Marryat, who was an actor in the scene, "like entering the gates of hell!"

The great floating mine drifted on through blackness and storm till, just as it struck the boom, Cochrane, who previously made his five assistants get into the boat, with his own hand lit the fuse and in turn jumped into the boat. How frantically the little crew pulled to get clear of the ignited mine may be imagined; but wind and sea were against them. The fuse, which was calculated to burn for twelve minutes, lasted for only five. Then the 1500 barrels of gunpowder went simultaneously off, peopling the black sky with a flaming torrent of shells, grenades, and rockets, and raising a mountainous wave that nearly swamped the unfortunate boat and its crew.

The fault of the fuse, however, saved the lives of the daring six, as the missiles from the exploding vessel fell far *outside* them. "The effect," says Cochrane, who, like Caesar, could write history as well as make it, "constituted one of the grandest artificial spectacles imaginable. For a moment the sky was red with the lurid glare arising from the simultaneous ignition of 1500 barrels of powder. On this gigantic flash subsiding the air seemed alive with shells, grenades, rockets, and masses of timber, the wreck of the shattered vessel."

Then came blackness, punctuated in flame by the explosion of the next floating mine. Then, through sea-wrack and night, came the squadron of fire-ships, each one a pyramid of kindling flame. But the first explosion had achieved all that Cochrane expected. It dismissed the huge boom into chips, and the French fleet lay open to attack. The captain of the second explosion vessel was so determined to do his work effectually that the entire crew was actually blown out of the vessel and one member of the party killed, while the toil of the boats in which, after the fire-ships had been abandoned, they and their crews had to fight their way back in the teeth of the gale, was so severe that several men died

of mere fatigue. The physical effects of the floating mines and the drifting fire-ships, as a matter of fact, were not very great. The boom, indeed, was destroyed, but out of twenty fire-ships only four actually reached the enemy's position, and not one did any damage. Cochrane's explosion vessels, however, were addressed not so much to the French ships as to the alarmed imagination of French sailors, and the effect achieved was overwhelming. All the French ships save one cut or slipped their cables, and ran ashore in wild confusion. Cochrane cut the moorings of his explosion vessel at half-past eight o'clock; by midnight, or in less than four hours, the boom had been destroyed, and thirteen French ships—the solitary fleet that remained to France—were lying helplessly ashore. Never, perhaps, was a result so great achieved in a time so brief, in a fashion so dramatic, or with a loss so trifling.

When the grey morning broke, with the exception of two vessels, the whole French fleet was lying helplessly aground on the Palles shoal. Some were lying on their bilge with the keel exposed, others were frantically casting their guns overboard and trying to get afloat again. Meanwhile Gambier and the British fleet were lying fourteen miles distant in the Basque Roads, and Cochrane in the *Impérieuse* was watching, with powder-blackened face, the curious spectacle of the entire fleet he had driven ashore, and the yet more amazing spectacle of a British fleet declining to come in and finally destroy its enemy. For here comes a chapter in the story on which Englishmen do not love to dwell. Cochrane tried to whip the muddy-spirited Gambier into enterprise by emphatic and quick-following signal. At six A.M. he signalled, *All the enemy's ships except two are on shore*, but this extracted from drowsy Gambier no other response than the answering pennant. Cochrane re-peated his impatient signals at half-hour intervals, and with emphasis ever more shrill.

The enemy's ships can be destroyed.
Half the fleet can destroy the enemy.
The frigates alone can destroy the enemy.

But still no response save the indifferent pennant. As the tide flowed in, the French ships showed signs of get-ting afloat, and Cochrane signalled, *The enemy is preparing to heave off,* even this brought no response from the pensive Gambier. At eleven o'clock the British fleet weighed and stood in, but then, to Cochrane's speechless wrath, re-an-chored at a distance of three and a half miles, and by this time two of the French three-deckers were afloat.

Gambier finally despatched a single mortar-vessel in to bombard the stranded ships, but by this time Cochrane had become desperate. He adopted a device which re-calls Nelson's use of his blind eye at Copenhagen. At one o'clock he hove his anchor atrip and drifted, stern fore-most, towards the enemy. He dare not make sail lest his trick should be detected and a signal of recall hoisted on the flagship. Cochrane coolly determined, in a word, to force the hand of his sluggish admiral. He drifted with his solitary frigate down to the hostile fleet and batter-ies, which Gambier thought it scarcely safe to attack with eleven ships of the line.

When near the enemy's position he suddenly made sail and ran up the signal, In want of assistance; next fol-lowed a yet more peremptory message, *In distress.* Even Gambier could not see an English frigate destroyed under the very guns of an English fleet without moving to its help, and he sent some of his ships in. But meanwhile,

Cochrane, though technically "in distress," was enjoying what he must have felt to be a singularly good time. He calmly took up a position which enabled him to engage an 80-gun ship, one of 74 guns, and, in particular, that French ship which, on the previous day, had hung the British flag under her quarter-gallery. For half-an-hour he fought these three ships single-handed, and the *Calcutta* actually struck to him, its captain afterwards being court-martialled and shot by the French themselves for surrendering to a frigate. Then the other British ships came up, and ship after ship of the French fleet struck or was destroyed. Night fell before the work was completed, and during the night Gambier, for some mysterious reason, recalled his ships; but Cochrane, in the *Impérieuse*, clung to his post. He persuaded Captain Seymour, in the *Pallas*, to remain with him, with four brigs, and with this tiny force he proposed to attack *L'Ocean*, the French flagship of 120 guns, which had just got afloat; but Gambier peremptorily recalled him at dawn, before the fight was renewed. Never before or since was a victory so complete and so nearly bloodless. Five seamen were killed in the fire-ships, and five in the attack on the French fleet and about twenty wounded; and with this microscopic "butcher's bill" a great fleet, the last naval hope of France, was practically destroyed. For so much does the genius and daring of a single man count!

That the French fleet was not utterly destroyed was due solely to Gambier's want of resolution. And yet, such is the irony of history, that of the two chief actors in this drama, Gambier, who marred it, was rewarded with the thanks of Parliament; Cochrane, who gave to it all its unique splendour, had his professional career abruptly terminated!

That wild night in the Aix Roads, and the solitary and daring attack on the French fleet which followed next day, were practically Cochrane's last acts as a British sailor. He achieved dazzling exploits under the flag of Chile and Brazil; but the most original warlike genius the English navy has ever known, fought no more battles for England.

CHAPTER 9

The *Shannon* and the *Chesapeake*

On the early morning of June 1, 1813, a solitary British frigate, H.M.S. *Shannon*, was cruising within sight of Boston lighthouse. She was a ship of about 1000 tons, and bore every mark of long and hard service. No gleam of colour sparkled about her. Her sides were rusty, her sails weather-stained; a solitary flag flew from her mizzen-peak, and even its blue had been bleached by sun and rain and wind to a dingy grey. A less romantic and more severely practical ship did not float, and her captain was of the same type as the ship.

Captain Philip Bowes Vere Broke was an Englishman *pur sang*, and of a type happily not uncommon. His fame will live as long as the British flag flies, yet a more sober and prosaic figure can hardly be imagined. He was not, like Nelson, a quarter-deck Napoleon; he had no gleam of Dundonald's matchless ruse de guerre. He was as deeply religious as Havelock or one of Cromwell's major-generals; he had the frugality of a Scotchman, and the heavy-footed common-sense of a Hollander. He was as nautical as a web-footed bird, and had no more "nerves" than a fish. A domestic Englishman, whose heart was always with the little girls at Brokehall, in Suffolk, but for whom the service of his country was a piety, and who might have competed with Lawrence for his self-chosen epitaph, "Here lies one who tried to do his duty."

A sober-suited, half-melancholy common-sense was Broke's characteristic, and he had applied it to the working of his ship, till he had made the vessel, perhaps, the most formidable fighting machine of her size afloat. He drilled his gunners until, from the swaying platform of their decks, they shot with a deadly coolness and accuracy nothing floating could resist. Broke, as a matter of fact, owed his famous victory over the *Chesapeake* to one of his matter of-fact precautions. The first broadside fired by the *Chesapeake* sent a 32-pound shot through one of the gun-room cabins into the magazine passage of the *Shannon*, where it might easily have ignited some grains of loose powder and blown the ship up, if Broke had not taken the precaution of elaborately *damping* that passage before the action began. The prosaic side of Broke's character is very amusing. In his diary he records his world-famous victory thus:—

"June 1st.—Off Boston. Moderate."

"N.W.—W(rote) Laurence."

"P.M.—Took *Chesapeake*."

Was ever a shining victory packed into fewer or duller words? Broke's scorn of the histrionic is shown by his reply to one of his own men who, when the *Chesapeake*, one blaze of fluttering colours, was bearing down upon her drab-coloured opponent, said to his commander, eyeing the bleached and solitary flag at the *Shannon's* peak, "Mayn't we have three ensigns, sir, like she has?" "No," said Broke, "we have always been an *unassuming* ship!"

And yet, this unromantic English sailor had a gleam of Don Quixote in him. On this pleasant summer morning he was waiting alone, under easy sail, outside a hostile port, strongly fortified and full of armed vessels, waiting for an enemy's ship bigger than himself to come out and fight him. He had sent in the previous day, by way of challenge, a letter that recalls the days of chivalry. "As the *Chesapeake*," he wrote to Laurence, its captain, "appears now ready for sea, I request that you will do me the favour to meet the *Shannon* with her, ship to ship." He proceeds to explain the exact armament of the *Shannon*, the number of her crew, the interesting circumstance that he is short of provisions and water, and that he has sent away his consort so that the terms of the duel may be fair. "If you will favour me," he says, "with any plan of signals or telegraph, I will warn you should any of my friends be too nigh, while you are in sight, until I can detach them out of the way. Or," he suggests coaxingly, "I would sail under a flag of truce to any place you think safest from our cruisers, hauling it down when fair, to begin hostilities. . . . Choose your terms," he concludes, "but let us meet." Having sent in this amazing letter, this middle-aged, unromantic, but hard-fighting captain climbs at daybreak to his own maintop, and sits there till half-past eleven, watching the challenged ship, to see if her foretopsail is unloosed and she is coming out to fight.

It is easy to understand the causes which kindled a British sailor of even Broke's unimaginative temperament into flame. On June 18, 1812, the United States, with magnificent audacity, declared war against Great Britain. England at that moment had 621 efficient cruisers at sea, 102 being line-of-battle ships. The American navy consisted of 8 frigates and 12 corvettes. It is true that England was at war at the same moment with half the civilised world; but what reasonable chance had the tiny naval power of the United States against the mighty fleets of England, commanded by men trained in the school of Nelson, and rich with the traditions of the Nile and Trafalgar? As a matter of fact, in the war which followed, the commerce of the United States was swept out of existence. But the Americans were of the same fighting stock as the English; to the Viking blood, indeed, they added Yankee ingenuity and resource, making a very formidable combination; and up to the June morning when the *Shannon* was waiting outside Boston Harbour for the *Chesapeake*, the naval honours of the war belonged to the Americans. The Americans had no fleet, and the campaign was one of single ship against single ship, but in these combats the Americans had scored more successes in twelve months than French seamen had gained in twelve years. The *Guerrière*, the *Java*, and the *Macedonian* had each been captured in single combat, and every British post-captain betwixt Portsmouth and Halifax was swearing with mere fury.

The Americans were shrewd enough to invent a new type of frigate which, in strength of frame, weight of metal, and general fighting power, was to a British frigate of the same class almost what an ironclad would be to a wooden ship. The *Constitution*, for example, was in size to the average British frigate as 15.3 to 10.9; in weight of metal as 76 to 51; and in crew as 46 to 25. Broke, however, had a well-founded belief in his ship and his men, and he proposed, in his sober fashion, to restore the tarnished honour of his flag by capturing single-handed the best American frigate afloat.

The *Chesapeake* was a fine ship, perfectly equipped, under a daring and popular commander. Laurence was a man of brilliant ingenuity and courage, and had won fame four months before by capturing in the *Hornet*, after a hard fight, the British brig-of-war *Peacock*. For this feat he had been promoted to the *Chesapeake*, and in his brief speech from

the quarterdeck just before the fight with the Shannon began, he called up the memory of the fight which made him
a popular hero by exhorting his crew to "*Peacock* her, my
lads! *Peacock* her!" The *Chesapeake* was larger than the *Shannon*, its crew was nearly a hundred men stronger, its weight
of fire 598 lbs. as against the *Shannon's* 538 lbs. Her guns
fired double-headed shot, and bars of wrought iron connected by links and loosely tied by a few rope yarns, which,
when discharged from the gun, spread out and formed a
flying iron chain six feet long. Its canister shot contained
jagged pieces of iron, broken bolts, and nails. As the British had a reputation for boarding, a large barrel of unslaked
lime was provided to fling in the faces of the boarders. An
early shot from the *Shannon*, by the way, struck this cask of
lime and scattered its contents in the faces of the Americans
themselves. Part of the equipment of the *Chesapeake* consisted of several hundred pairs of handcuffs, intended for
the wrists of English prisoners. Boston citizens prepared a
banquet in honour of the victors for the same evening, and
a small fleet of pleasure-boats followed the *Chesapeake* as
she came gallantly out to the fight.

Never was a braver, shorter, or more murderous fight.
Laurence, the most gallant of men, bore steadily down,
without firing a shot, to the starboard quarter of the *Shannon*. When within fifty yards he luffed; his men sprang
into the shrouds and gave three cheers. Broke fought with
characteristic silence and composure. He forbade his men
to cheer, enforced the sternest silence along his deck, and
ordered the captain of each gun to fire as his piece bore
on the enemy. "Fire into her quarters," he said, "main-deck
into main-deck, quarter-deck into quarter-deck. Kill the
men, and the ship is yours."

The sails of the *Chesapeake* swept betwixt the slanting rays of the evening sun and the *Shannon*, the drifting shadow darkened the English main-deck ports, the rush of the enemy's cut-water could be heard through the grim silence of the *Shannon's* decks. Suddenly there broke out the first gun from the *Shannon*; then her whole side leaped into flame. Never was a more fatal broadside discharged. A tempest of shot, splinters, torn hammocks, cut rigging, and wreck of every kind was hurled like a cloud across the deck of the *Chesapeake*, and of one hundred and fifty men at stations there, more than a hundred were killed or wounded. A more fatal loss to the Americans instantly followed, as Captain Laurence, the fiery soul of his ship, was shot through the abdomen by an English marine, and fell mortally wounded.

The answering thunder of the *Chesapeake's* guns, of course, rolled out, and then, following quick, the overwhelming blast of the *Shannon's* broadside once more. Each ship, indeed, fired two full broadsides, and, as the guns fell quickly out of range, part of another broadside. The firing of the *Chesapeake* was furious and deadly enough to have disabled an ordinary ship. It is computed that forty effective shots would be enough to disable a frigate; the *Shannon* during the six minutes of the firing was struck by no less than 158 shot, a fact which proves the steadiness and power of the American fire. But the fire of the *Shannon* was overwhelming. In those same six fatal minutes she smote the *Chesapeake* with no less than 362 shots, an average of 60 shots of all sizes every minute, as against the *Chesapeake's* 28 shots. The *Chesapeake* was fir-built, and the British shot riddled her. One *Shannon* broadside partly raked the *Chesapeake* and literally smashed the stern cab-

ins and battery to mere splinters, as completely as though a procession of aerolites had torn through it.

The swift, deadly, concentrated fire of the British in two quick-following broadsides practically decided the combat. The partially disabled vessels drifted together, and the *Chesapeake* fell on board the *Shannon*, her quarter striking the starboard main-chains. Broke, as the ships ground together, looked over the blood-splashed decks of the American and saw the men deserting the quarter-deck guns, under the terror of another broadside at so short a distance. "Follow me who can," he shouted, and with characteristic coolness "stepped"—in his own phrase—across the *Chesapeake's* bulwark. He was followed by some 32 seamen and 18 marines—50 British boarders leaping upon a ship with a crew of 400 men, a force which, even after the dreadful broadsides of the *Shannon*, still numbered 270 unwounded men in its ranks.

It is absurd to deny to the Americans courage of the very finest quality, but the amazing and unexpected severity of the *Shannon's* fire had destroyed for the moment their *morale*, and the British were in a mood of victory. The boatswain of the *Shannon*, an old *Rodney* man, lashed the two ships together, and in the act had his left arm literally hacked off by repeated strokes of a cutlass and was killed. One British midshipman, followed by five topmen, crept along the *Shannon's* foreyard and stormed the *Chesapeake's* foretop, killing the men stationed there, and then swarmed down by a back-stay to join the fighting on the deck. Another middy tried to attack the *Chesapeake's* mizzentop from the starboard mainyard arm, but being hindered by the foot of the topsail, stretched himself out on the mainyard arm, and from that post shot three of the enemy in succession.

Meanwhile the fight on the deck had been short and sharp; some of the Americans leaped overboard and others rushed below; and Laurence, lying wounded in his steerage, saw the wild reflux of his own men down the after ladders. On asking what it meant, he was told, "The ship is boarded, and those are the *Chesapeake's* men driven from the upper decks by the English." This so exasperated the dying man that he called out repeatedly, "Then blow her up; blow her up."

The fight lasted exactly thirteen minutes—the broadsides occupied six minutes, the boarding seven—and in thirteen minutes after the first shot the British flag was flying over the American ship. The *Shannon* and *Chesapeake* were bearing up, side by side, for Halifax. The spectators in the pleasure-boats were left ruefully staring at the spectacle; those American handcuffs, so thoughtfully provided, were on American wrists; and the Boston citizens had to consume, with what appetite they might, their own banquet. The carnage on the two ships was dreadful. In thirteen minutes 252 men were either killed or wounded, an average of nearly twenty men for every minute the fight lasted. In the combat betwixt these two frigates, in fact, nearly as many men were struck down as in the whole battle of Navarino! The *Shannon* itself lost as many men as any 74-gun ship ever lost in battle.

Judge Haliburton, famous as "Sam Slick," when a youth of seventeen, boarded the *Chesapeake* as the two battered ships sailed into Halifax. "The deck," he wrote, "had not been cleaned, and the coils and folds of rope were steeped in gore as if in a slaughter-house. Pieces of skin with pendent hair were adhering to the sides of the ship; and in one place I noticed portions of fingers protruding, as if thrust through the outer walls of the frigate."

Watts, the first lieutenant of the *Shannon*, was killed by the fire of his own ship in a very remarkable manner. He boarded with his captain, with his own hands pulled down the *Chesapeake's* flag, and hastily bent on the halliards the English ensign, as he thought, above the Stars and Stripes, and then rehoisted it. In the hurry he had bent the English flag under the Stars and Stripes instead of above it, and the gunners of the *Shannon*, seeing the American stripes going up first, opened fire instantly on the group at the foot of the mizzen-mast, blew the top of their own unfortunate lieutenant's head off with a grape shot, and killed three or four of their own men.

Captain Broke was desperately wounded in a curious fashion. A group of Americans, who had laid down their arms, saw the British captain standing for a moment alone on the break of the forecastle. It seemed a golden chance. They snatched up weapons lying on the deck, and leaped upon him. Warned by the shout of the sentry, Broke turned round to find three of the enemy with uplifted weapons rushing on him. He parried the middle fellow's pike and wounded him in the face, but was instantly struck down with a blow from the butt-end of a musket, which laid bare his skull. He also received a slash from the cutlass of the third man, which clove a portion of skull completely away and left the brain bare. He fell, and was grappled on the deck by the man he had first wounded, a powerful fellow, who got uppermost and raised a bayonet to thrust through Broke. At this moment a British marine came running up, and concluding that the man underneath must be an American, also raised his bayonet to give the *coup de grace*. "Pooh, pooh, you fool," said Broke in the most matter-of-fact fashion, "don't you know your captain?" whereupon the marine changed the direction of his thrust and slew the American.

The news reached London on July 7, and was carried straight to the House of Commons, where Lord Cochrane was just concluding a fierce denunciation of the Admiralty on the ground of the disasters suffered from the Americans, and Croker, the Secretary to the Admiralty, was able to tell the story of the fight off Boston to the wildly cheering House, as a complete defence of his department. Broke was at once created a Baronet and a Knight of the Bath. In America, on the other hand, the story of the fight was received with mingled wrath and incredulity. "I remember," says Rush, afterwards U.S. Minister at the Court of St. James, "at the first rumour of it, the universal incredulity. I remember how the post-offices were thronged for successive days with anxious thousands; how collections of citizens rode out for miles on the highway to get the earliest news the mail brought. At last, when the certainty was known, I remember the public gloom, the universal badges of mourning. 'Don't give up the ship,' the dying words of Laurence, were on every tongue."

It was a great fight, the most memorable and dramatic sea-duel in naval history. The combatants were men of the same stock, and fought with equal bravery. Both nations, in fact, may be proud of a fight so frank, so fair, so gallant. The world, we may hope, will never witness another *Shannon* engaged in the fierce wrestle of battle with another *Chesapeake*, for the Union Jack and the Stars and Stripes are knitted together by a bond woven of common blood and speech and political ideals that grows stronger every year.

For years the *Shannon* and the *Chesapeake* lay peacefully side by side in the Medway, and the two famous ships might well have been preserved as trophies. The *Chesapeake* was bought by the Admiralty after the fight for exactly £21,314-11s-11¼d., and six years afterwards she was sold as mere old timber for 500 pounds, was broken up, and to-day stands as a Hampshire flour-mill, peacefully grinding English corn; but still on the mill-timbers can be seen the marks of the grape and round shot of the *Shannon*.

CHAPTER 10

Great Sea-Duels

British naval history is rich in the records of what may be called great sea-duels—combats, that is, of single ship against single ship, waged often with extraordinary fierceness and daring. They resemble the combat of knight against knight, with flash of cannon instead of thrust of lance, and the floor of the lonely sea for the trampled lists.

He must have a very slow-beating imagination who cannot realise the picturesqueness of these ancient sea-duels. Two frigates cruising for prey catch the far-off gleam of each other's topsails over the rim of the horizon. They approach each other warily, two high-sniffing sea-mastiffs. A glimpse of fluttering colour—the red flag and the *drapeau blanc*, or the Union Jack and the tricolour—reveals to each ship its foe. The men stand grimly at quarters; the captain, with perhaps a solitary lieutenant, and a middy as aide-de-camp, is on his quarter-deck. There is the manoeuvring for the weather-gage, the thunder of the sudden broadside, the hurtle and crash of the shot, the stern, quick word of command as the clumsy guns are run in to be reloaded and fired again and again with furious haste. The ships drift into closer wrestle. Masts and yards come tumbling on to the blood-splashed decks. There is the grinding shock of the great wooden hulls as they meet, the wild leap of the boarders, the clash of cutlass on cutlass, the shout of victory, the sight of the fluttering flag as it sinks reluctantly from the mizzen of the beaten ship. Then the smoke drifts away, and on the tossing sea-floor lie, little better than dismantled wrecks, victor and vanquished.

No great issue, perhaps, ever hung upon these lonely sea-combats; but as object-lessons in the qualities by which the empire has been won, and by which it must be maintained, these ancient sea-fights have real and permanent value. What better examples of cool hardihood, of chivalrous loyalty to the flag, of self-reliant energy, need be imagined or desired? The generation that carries the heavy burden of the empire to-day cannot afford to forget the tale of such exploits.

One of the most famous frigate fights in British history is that between the *Arethusa* and *La Belle Poule*, fought off Brest on June 17, 1778. Who is not familiar with the name and fame of "the saucy *Arethusa*"? Yet there is a curious absence of detail as to the fight. The combat, indeed, owes its enduring fame to two somewhat irrelevant circumstances—first, that it was fought when France and England were not actually at war, but were trembling on the verge of it. The sound of the *Arethusa's* guns, indeed, was the signal of war between the two nations. The other fact is that an ingenious rhymester—scarcely a poet—crystal-lised the fight into a set of verses in which there is something of the true smack of the sea, and an echo, if not of the cannon's roar, yet of the rough-voiced mirth of the forecastle; and the sea-fight lies embalmed, so to speak, and made immortal in the sea-song.

The *Arethusa* was a stumpy little frigate, scanty in crew, light in guns, attached to the fleet of Admiral Keppel, then cruising off Brest. Keppel had as perplexed and delicate a charge as was ever entrusted to a British admiral. Great Britain was at war with her American colonies, and there was every sign that France intended to add herself to the fight. No fewer than thirty-two sail of the line and twelve frigates were gathered in Brest roads, and another fleet of almost equal strength in Toulon. Spain, too, was slowly collecting a mighty armament. What would happen to England if the Toulon and Brest fleets united, were joined by a third fleet from Spain, and the mighty array of ships thus collected swept up the British Channel? On June 13, 1778, Keppel, with twenty-one ships of the line and three frigates, was despatched to keep watch over the Brest fleet. War had not been proclaimed, but Keppel was to prevent a junction of the Brest and Toulon fleets, by persuasion if he could, but by gunpowder in the last resort.

Keppel's force was much inferior to that of the Brest fleet, and as soon as the topsails of the British ships were visible from the French coast, two French frigates, the *Licorne* and *La Belle Poule*, with two lighter craft, bore down upon them to reconnoitre. But Keppel could not afford to let the French admiral know his exact force, and signalled to his own outlying ships to bring the French frigates under his lee.

At nine o'clock at night the *Licorne* was overtaken by the *Milford*, and with some rough sailorly persuasion, and a hint of broadsides, her head was turned towards the British fleet. The next morning, in the grey dawn, the Frenchman, having meditated on affairs during the night, made a wild dash for freedom. The *America*, an English 64—double, that is, the *Licorne's* size—overtook her, and fired a shot across her bow to bring her to. Longford, the captain of the *America*, stood on the gunwale of his own ship politely urging the captain of the *Licorne* to return with him. With a burst of

Celtic passion the French captain fired his whole broadside into the big Englishman, and then instantly hauled down his flag so as to escape any answering broadside! Meanwhile the *Arethusa* was in eager pursuit of the *Belle Poule*; a fox-terrier chasing a mastiff! The *Belle Poule* was a splendid ship, with heavy metal, and a crew more than twice as numerous as that of the tiny *Arethusa*. But Marshall, its captain, was a singularly gallant sailor, and not the man to count odds. The song tells the story of the fight in an amusing fashion:

> *Come all ye jolly sailors bold,*
> *Whose hearts are cast in honour's mould,*
> *While England's glory I unfold.*
> *Huzza to the* Arethusa!
> *She is a frigate tight and brave*
> *As ever stemmed the dashing wave;*
> *Her men are staunch*
> *To their fav'rite launch,*
> *And when the foe shall meet our fire,*
> *Sooner than strike we'll all expire*
> *On board the* Arethusa.
>
> *On deck five hundred men did dance,*
> *The stoutest they could find in France;*
> *We, with two hundred, did advance*
> *On board the* Arethusa.
> *Our captain hailed the Frenchman, 'Ho!'*
> *The Frenchman then cried out, 'Hallo!'*
> *'Bear down, d'ye see,*
> *To our Admiral's lee.'*
> *'No, no,' says the Frenchman, 'that can't be.*
> *'Then I must lug you along with me,'*
> *Says the saucy* Arethusa!

As a matter of fact Marshall hung doggedly on the Frenchman's quarter for two long hours, fighting a ship twice as big as his own. The *Belle Poule* was eager to escape; Marshall was resolute that it should not escape; and, try as he might, the Frenchman, during that fierce two hours' wrestle, failed to shake off his tiny but dogged antagonist. The *Arethusa's* masts were shot away, its jib-boom hung a tangled wreck over its bows, its bulwarks were shattered, its decks were splashed red with blood, half its guns were dismounted, and nearly every third man in its crew struck down. But still it hung, with quench-less and obstinate courage, on the *Belle Poule's* quarter, and by its perfect seamanship and the quickness and the deadly precision with which its lighter guns worked, re-duced its towering foe to a condition of wreck almost as complete as its own. The terrier, in fact, was proving too much for the mastiff.

Suddenly the wind fell. With topmasts hanging over the side, and canvas torn to ribbons, the *Arethusa* lay shat-tered and moveless on the sea. The shot-torn but loftier sails of the *Belle Poule*, however, yet held wind enough to drift her out of the reach of the *Arethusa* fire. Both ships were close under the French cliffs; but the *Belle Poule*, like a broken-winged bird, struggled into a tiny cove in the rocks, and nothing remained for the *Arethusa* but to cut away her wreckage, hoist what sail she could, and drag herself sullenly back under jury-masts to the British fleet. But the story of that two hours' heroic fight maintained against such odds sent a thrill of grim exultation through Great Britain. Menaced by the combination of so many mighty states, while her sea-dogs were of this fighting temper, what had Great Britain to fear? In the streets of many a British seaport, and in many a British forecastle, the story of how the *Arethusa* fought was sung in deep-throated chorus:

The fight was off the Frenchman's land;
We forced them back upon their strand;
For we fought till not a stick would stand
Of the gallant Arethusa!

A fight even more dramatic in its character is that fought on August 10, 1805, between the *Phoenix* and the *Didon*. The *Didon* was one of the finest and fastest French frigates afloat, armed with guns of special calibre and manned by a crew which formed, perhaps, the very *élite* of the French navy. The men had been specially picked to form the crew of the only French ship which was commanded by a Bonaparte, the *Pomone*, selected for the command of Captain Jerome Bonaparte. Captain Jerome Bonaparte, however, was not just now afloat, and the *Didon* had been selected, on account of its great speed and heavy armament, for a service of great importance. She was manned by the crew chosen for the *Pomone*, placed under an officer of special skill and daring—Captain Milias—and despatched with orders for carrying out one more of those naval "combinations" which Napoleon often attempted, but never quite accomplished. The *Didon*, in a word, was to bring up the Rochefort squadron to join the Franco-Spanish fleet under Villeneuve.

On that fatal August 10, however, it seemed to Captain Milias that fortune had thrust into his hands a golden opportunity of snapping up a British sloop of war, and carrying her as a trophy into Rochefort. An American merchantman fell in with him, and its master reported that he had been brought-to on the previous day by a British man-of-war, and compelled to produce his papers. The American told the French captain that he had been allowed to go round the Englishman's decks and count his guns—omitting, no doubt, to add that he was half-drunk while doing it. Contemplated through an American's prejudices, inflamed with grog, the British ship seemed a very poor thing indeed. She carried, the American told the captain of the *Didon*, only twenty guns of light calibre, and her captain and officers were "so cocky" that if they had a chance they would probably lay themselves alongside even the *Didon* and become an easy prey. The American pointed out to the eagerly listening Frenchmen the topgallant sails of the ship he was describing showing above the sky-line to windward. Captain Milias thought he saw glory and cheap victory beckoning him, and he put his helm down, and stood under easy sail towards the fast-rising topsails of the Englishman.

Now, the *Phoenix* was, perhaps, the smallest frigate in the British navy; a stocky little craft, scarcely above the rating of a sloop; and its captain, Baker, a man with something of Dundonald's gift for ruse, had disguised his ship so as to look as much as possible like a sloop. Baker, too, who believed that light guns quickly handled were capable of more effective mischief than the slow fire of heavier guns, had changed his heavier metal for 18-pounders. The two ships, therefore, were very unequal in fighting force. The broadside of the *Didon* was nearly fifty per cent. heavier than that of the *Phoenix*; her crew was nearly fifty per cent. more numerous, and she was splendidly equipped at every point.

The yellow sides and royal yards rigged aloft told the "cocky" *Phoenix* that the big ship to leeward was a

Frenchman, and, with all sails spread, she bore down in the chase. Baker was eager to engage his enemy to leeward, that she might not escape, and he held his fire till he could reach the desired position. The *Didon*, however, a quick and weatherly ship, was able to keep ahead of the *Phoenix*, and thrice poured in a heavy broadside upon the grimly silent British ship without receiving a shot in reply. Baker's men were falling fast at their quarters, and, impatient at being both foiled and raked, he at last ran fiercely at his enemy to windward. The heads of both ships swung parallel, and at pistol-distance broadside furiously answered broadside. In order to come up with her opponent, however, the *Phoenix* had all sail spread, and she gradually forged ahead. As soon as the two ships were clear, the *Didon*, by a fine stroke of seamanship, hauled up, crossed the stern of the *Phoenix*, and raked her, and then repeated the pleasant operation. The rigging of the *Phoenix* was so shattered that for a few minutes she was out of hand. Baker, however, was a fine seaman, and his crew were in a high state of discipline; and when the *Didon* once more bore up to rake her antagonist, the British ship, with her sails thrown aback, evaded the Frenchman's fire. But the stern of the *Didon* smote with a crash on the starboard quarter of the Phoenix; the ships were lying parallel; the broadside of neither could be brought to bear. The Frenchmen, immensely superior in numbers, made an impetuous rush across their forecastle, and leaped on the quarter-deck of the *Phoenix*. The marines of that ship, however, drawn up in a steady line across the deck, resisted the whole rush of the French boarders; and the British sailors, tumbling up from their guns, cutlass and boarding-pike in hand, and wroth with the audacity of the "French lubbers" daring to board the "cocky little *Phoenix*," with one rush, pushed fiercely home, swept the Frenchmen back on to their own vessel.

On the French forecastle stood a brass 36-pounder carronade; this commanded the whole of the British ship, and with it the French opened a most destructive fire. The British ship, as it happened, could not bring a single gun to bear in return. Baker, however, had fitted the cabin window on either quarter of his ship to serve as a port, in preparation for exactly such a contingency as this; and the aftermost main-deck gun was dragged into the cabin, the improvised port thrown open, and Baker himself, with a cluster of officers and men, was eagerly employed in fitting tackles to enable the gun to be worked. As the sides of the two ships were actually grinding together the Frenchmen saw the preparations being made; a double squad of marines was brought up at a run to the larboard gangway, and opened a swift and deadly fire into the cabin, crowded with English sailors busy rigging their gun. The men dropped in clusters; the floor of the cabin was covered with the slain, its walls were splashed with blood. But Baker and the few men not yet struck down kept coolly to their task. The gun was loaded under the actual flash of the French muskets, its muzzle was thrust through the port, and it was fired! Its charge of langrage swept the French ship from her larboard bow to her starboard quarter, and struck down in an instant twenty-four men. The deadly fire was renewed again and again, the British marines on the quarter-deck meanwhile keeping down with their musketry the fire of the great French carronade.

That fierce and bloody wrestle lasted for nearly thirty minutes, then the *Didon* began to fore-reach. Her great bowsprit ground slowly along the side of the *Phoenix*. It crossed the line of the second aftermost gun on the British main-deck. Its flames on the instant smote the Frenchman's head-rails to splinters, and destroyed the gammoning of her bowsprit. Gun after gun of the two ships was brought in succession to bear; but in this close and deadly contest the *Phoenix* had the advantage. Her guns were lighter, her men better drilled, and their fierce energy overbore the French-men. Presently the *Didon*, with her foremast tottering, her maintopmast gone, her decks a blood-stained wreck, passed out of gunshot ahead.

In the tangle between the two ships the fly of the British white ensign at the gaff end dropped on the *Didon* forecastle. The Frenchmen tore it off, and, as the ships moved apart, they waved it triumphantly from the *Didon* stern. All the colours of the *Phoenix*, indeed, in one way or another had vanished, and the only response the exasperated British tars could make to the insult of the *Didon* was to immediately lash a boat's ensign to the larboard, and the Union Jack to the starboard end of their cross jack yard-arm.

The wind had dropped; both ships were now lying a in a semi-wrecked condition out of gunshot of each other, and it became a question of which could soonest repair damages and get into fighting condition again. Both ships, as it happened, had begun the fight with nearly all canvas spread, and from their splintered masts the sails now hung one wild network of rags. In each ship a desperate race to effect repairs began. On the Frenchman's decks arose a Babel of sounds, the shouts of officers, the tumult of the men's voices. The British, on the other hand, worked in grim and orderly silence, with no sound but the cool, stern orders of the officers. In such a race the British were sure to win, and fortune aided them. The two ships were rolling heavily in the windless swell, and a little before noon the British saw the wounded foremast of their enemy suddenly snap and tumble, with all its canvas, upon the unfortunate *Didon's* decks. This gave new and exultant vigour to the British. Shot-holes were plugged, dismounted guns refitted, fresh braces rove, the torn rigging spliced, new canvas spread. The wind blew softly again, and a little after noon the *Phoenix*, sorely battered indeed, but in fighting trim, with guns loaded, and the survivors of her crew at quarters, bore down on the *Didon*, and took her position on that ship's weather bow. Just when the word "Fire!" was about to be given, the *Didon's* flag fluttered reluctantly down; she had struck!

The toils of the *Phoenix*, however, were not even yet ended. The ship she had captured was practically a wreck, its mainmast tottering to its fall, while the prisoners greatly exceeded in numbers their captors. The little *Phoenix* courageously took her big prize in tow, and laid her course for Plymouth. Once the pair of crippled frigates were chased by the whole of Villeneuve's fleet; once, by a few chance words overheard, a plot amongst the French prisoners for seizing the *Phoenix* and then retaking the *Didon* was detected—almost too late—and thwarted. The *Phoenix*, and her prize too, reached Gibraltar when a thick fog lay on the straits, a fog which, as the sorely damaged ships crept through it, was full of the sound of signal guns and the ringing of bells. The Franco-Spanish fleet, in a word, a procession of giants, went slowly past the crippled ships in the fog, and never saw them!

On September 3, however, the *Phoenix* safely brought her hard-won and stubborn-guarded prize safely into Plymouth Sound.

The fight between the two ships was marked by many heroic incidents. During the action the very invalids in the sick-bay of the *Phoenix* crept from their cots and tried to take some feeble part in the fight. The purser is not usually part of the fighting staff of a ship, but the acting purser of the *Phoenix*, while her captain was in the smoke-filled cabin below, trying to rig up a gun to bear on the *Didon*, took charge of the quarter-deck, kept his post right opposite the brazen mouth of the great carronade we have described, and, with a few marines, kept down the fire. A little middy had the distinction of saving his captain's life. The *Didon's* bowsprit was thrust, like the shaft of a gigantic lance, over the quarter of the *Phoenix*, and a Frenchman, lying along it, levelled his musket at Captain Baker, not six paces distant, and took deliberate aim. A middy named Phillips, armed with a musket as big as himself, saw the levelled piece of the Frenchman; he gave his captain an unceremonious jostle aside just as the Frenchman's musket flashed, and with almost the same movement discharged his own piece at the enemy. The French bullet tore off the rim of Captain Baker's hat, but the body of the man who fired it fell with a splash betwixt the two ships into the water. Here was a story, indeed, for a middy to tell, to the admiration of all the gun-rooms in the fleet.

The middy of the period, however, was half imp, half hero. Another youthful Nelson, *aetat.* sixteen, at the hottest stage of the fight—probably at the moment the acting-purser was in command on the quarter-deck—found an opportunity of getting at the purser's stores. With jaws

widely distended, he was in the act of sucking—in the fashion so delightful to boys—a huge orange, when a musket ball, after passing through the head of a seaman, went
clean through both the youth's distended cheeks, and this
without touching a single tooth. Whether this affected the
flavour of the orange is not told, but the historian gravely
records that "when the wound in each cheek healed, a pair
of not unseemly dimples remained" Happy middy! He
would scarcely envy Nelson his peerage.

CHAPTER 11

Famous Cutting-Out Expeditions

As illustrations of cool daring, of the courage that does not count numbers or depend on noise, nor flinch from flame or steel, few things are more wonderful than the many cutting-out stories to be found in the history of the British navy. The soldier in the forlorn hope, scrambling up the breach swept by grape and barred by a triple line of steadfast bayonets, must be a brave man. But it may be doubted whether he shows a courage so cool and high as that of a boat's crew of sailors in a cutting-out expedition.

The ship to be attacked lies, perhaps, floating in a tropic haze five miles off, and the attacking party must pull slowly, in a sweltering heat, up to the iron lips of her guns. The greedy, restless sea is under them, and a single shot may turn the eager boat's crew at any instant into a cluster of drowning wretches. When the ship is reached, officers and men must clamber over bulwarks and boarding-netting, exposed, almost helplessly, as they climb, to thrust of pike and shot of musket, and then leap down, singly and without order, on to the deck crowded with foes. Or, perhaps, the ship to be cut out lies in a hostile port under the guard of powerful batteries, and the boats must dash in through the darkness, and their crews tumble, at three or four separate points, on to the deck of the foe, cut her

161

cables, let fall her sails, and—while the mad fight still rages on her deck and the great battery booms from the cliff overhead—carry the ship out of the harbour. These, surely, are deeds of which only a sailor's courage is capable! Let a few such stories be taken from faded naval records and told afresh to a new generation.

In July 1800 the 14-gun cutter *Viper*, commanded by acting Lieutenant Jeremiah Coghlan, was attached to Sir Edward Pellew's squadron off Port Louis. Coghlan, as his name tells, was of Irish blood. He had just emerged from the chrysalis stage of a midshipman, and, flushed with the joy of an independent command, was eager for adventure. The entrance to Port Louis was watched by a number of gunboats constantly on sentry-go, and Coghlan conceived the idea of jumping suddenly on one of these, and carrying her off from under the guns of the enemy's fleet. He persuaded Sir Edward Pellew to lend him the flagship's ten-oared cutter, with twelve volunteers. Having got this reinforcement, and having persuaded the *Amethyst* frigate to lend him a boat and crew, Mr. Jeremiah Coghlan proceeded to carry out another and very different plan from that he had ventured to suggest to his admiral. A French gun-brig, named the *Cerbère*, was lying in the harbour of St. Louis. She mounted three long 24 and four 6-pounders, and was moored, with springs in her cables, within pistol-shot of three batteries. A French seventy-four and two frigates were within gunshot of her. She had a crew of eighty-six men, sixteen of whom were soldiers. It was upon this brig, lying under three powerful batteries, within a hostile and difficult port, that Mr. Jeremiah Coghlan proposed, in the darkness of night, to make a dash. He added the *Viper's* solitary midshipman, with himself and six of his crew, to the twelve volunteers on board the flagship's cutter, raising its crew to twenty men, and, with the *Amethyst's* boat and a small boat from the *Viper*, pulled off in the blackness of the night on this daring adventure.

The ten-oared cutter ran away from the other two boats, reached the *Cerbère*, found her with battle lanterns alight and men at quarters, and its crew at once jumped on board the Frenchman. Coghlan, as was proper, jumped first, landed on a trawl-net hung up to dry, and, while sprawling helpless in its meshes, was thrust through the thigh with a pike, and with his men—several also severely hurt—tumbled back into the boat. The British picked themselves up, hauled their boat a little farther ahead, clambered up the sides of the *Cerbère* once more, and were a second time beaten back with new wounds. They clung to the Frenchman, however, fought their way up to a new point, broke through the French defences, and after killing or wounding twenty-six of the enemy—or more than every fourth man of the *Cerbère's* crew—actually captured her, the other two boats coming up in time to help in towing out the prize under a wrathful fire from the batteries. Coghlan had only one killed and eight wounded, himself being wounded in two places, and his middy in six. Sir Edward Pellew, in his official despatch, grows eloquent over "the courage which, hand to hand, gave victory to a handful of brave fellows over four times their number, and the skill which planned, conducted, and effected so daring an enterprise." Earl St. Vincent, himself the driest and grimmest of admirals, was so delighted with the youthful Irishman's exploit that he presented him with a handsome sword.

In 1811, again, Great Britain was at war with the Dutch—a tiny little episode of the great revolutionary

war. A small squadron of British ships was cruising off
Batavia. A French squadron, with troops to strengthen the
garrison, was expected daily. The only fortified port into
which they could run was Marrack, and the commander
of the British squadron cruising to intercept the French
ships determined to make a dash by night on Marrack, and
so secure the only possible landing-place for the French.
Marrack was defended by batteries mounting fifty-four
heavy guns. The attacking force was to consist of 200 seamen and 250 troops, under the command of Lieutenant
Lyons of the *Minden*. Just before the boats pushed off,
however, the British commander learned that the Dutch
garrison had been heavily reinforced, and deeming an assault too hazardous, the plan was abandoned. A few days
afterwards Lyons, with the *Minden's* launch and cutter, was
despatched to land nineteen prisoners at Batavia, and pick
up intelligence. Lyons, a very daring and gallant officer,
learned that the Marrack garrison was in a state of sleepy
security, and, with his two boats' crews, counting thirty-
five officers and men, he determined to make a midnight
dash on the fort, an exploit which 430 men were reckoned too weak a force to attempt.

Lyons crept in at sunset to the shore, and hid his two
boats behind a point from which the fort was visible. A little after midnight, just as the moon dipped below the horizon, Lyons stole with muffled oars round the point, and
instantly the Dutch sentries gave the alarm. Lyons, however,
pushed fiercely on, grounded his boats in a heavy surf under the very embrasures of the lower battery, and, in an
instant, thirty-five British sailors were tumbling over the
Dutch guns and upon the heavy-breeched and astonished
Dutch gunners. The battery was carried. Lyons gathered his

thirty-five sailors into a cluster, and, with a rush, captured the upper battery. Still climbing up, they reached the top of the hill, and found the whole Dutch garrison forming in line to receive them. The sailors instantly ran in upon the half-formed line, cutlass in hand; Lyons roared that he "had 400 men, and would give no quarter;" and the Dutch, finding the pace of events too rapid for their nerves, broke and fled. But the victorious British were only thirty-five in number, and were surrounded by powerful forces. They began at once to dismantle the guns and destroy the fort, but two Dutch gunboats in the bay opened fire on them, as did a heavy battery in the rear.

At daybreak a strong Dutch column was formed, and came on at a resolute and laborious trot towards the shattered gate of the fort. Lyons had trained two 24-pounders, loaded to the muzzle with musket balls, on the gate, left invitingly open. He himself stood, with lighted match, by one gun; his second in command, with another lighted match, by the other. They waited coolly by the guns till the Dutch, their officers leading, reached the gate, raising a tumult of angry guttural shouts as they came on. Then, from a distance of little over ten yards, the British fired. The head of the column was instantly smashed, its tail broken up into flying fragments. Lyons finished the destruction of the fort at leisure, sank one of the two gunboats with the last shot fired from the last gun before he spiked it, and marched off, leaving the British flag flying on the staff above the fort, where, in the fury of the attack, it had been hoisted in a most gallant fashion by the solitary middy of the party, a lad named Franks, only fifteen years old. One of the two boats belonging to the British had been bilged by the surf, and the thirty-five seamen—only four of them wounded—

packed themselves into the remaining boat and pulled off, carrying with them the captured Dutch colours. Let the reader's imagination illuminate, as the writer's pen cannot, that midnight dash by thirty-five men on a heavily armed fort with a garrison twelve times the strength of the attacking force. Where in stories of warfare, ancient or modern, is such another tale of valour to be found? Lyons, however, was not promoted, as he had "acted without orders."

A tale, with much the same flavour in it, but not so dramatically successful, has for its scene the coast of Spain. In August 1812, the British sloop *Minstrel*, of 24 guns, and the 18-gun brig *Philomel*, were blockading three small French privateers in the port of Biendom, near Alicante. The privateers were protected by a strong fort mounting 24 guns. By way of precaution, two of the ships were hauled on shore, six of their guns being landed, and formed into a battery manned by eighty of their crews. The *Minstrel* and her consort could not pretend to attack a position so strong, but they kept vigilant watch outside, and a boat from one ship or the other rowed guard every night near the shore. On the night of the 12th the *Minstrel's* boat, with seven seamen, was in command of an Irish midshipman named Michael Dwyer. Dwyer had all the fighting courage of his race, with almost more of the gay disregard of odds than is natural to even an Irish midshipman. It occurred to Mr. Michael Dwyer that if he could carry by surprise the 6-gun battery, there would be a chance of destroying the privateers. A little before ten P.M. he pulled silently to the beach, at a point three miles distant from the battery, and, with his seven followers, landed, and was instantly challenged by a French sentry. Dwyer by some accident knew Spanish, and, with ready-witted audacity, replied in that language that "they were peasants." They were allowed to pass, and these seven tars, headed by a youth, set off on the three miles' trudge to attack a fort!

There were eighty men in the battery when Michael and his amazing seven rushed upon it. There was a wild struggle for five minutes, and then the eighty fled before the eight, and the delighted middy found himself in possession of the battery. But the alarm was given, and two companies of French infantry, each one hundred strong, came resolutely up to retake the battery. Eight against eighty seemed desperate odds, but eight against two hundred is a quite hopeless proportion. Yet Mr. Dwyer and his seven held the fort till one of their number was killed, two (including the midshipman) badly wounded, and, worst of all, their ammunition exhausted. When the British had fired their last shot, the French, with levelled bayonets, broke in; but the inextinguishable Dwyer was not subdued till he had been stabbed in seventeen places, and of the whole eight British only one was left unwounded. The French amazement when they discovered that the force which attacked them consisted of seven men and a boy, was too deep for words.

Perhaps the most brilliant cutting-out in British records is the carrying of the *Chevrette* by the boats of three British frigates in Cameret Bay in 1801. A previous and mismanaged attempt had put the *Chevrette* on its guard; it ran a mile and a half farther up the bay, moored itself under some heavy batteries, took on board a powerful detachment of infantry, bringing its number of men up to 339, and then hoisted in defiance a large French ensign over the British flag. Some temporary redoubts were thrown up on the points of land commanding the *Chevrette*, and a heavily armed gunboat was moored at the entrance of the bay as a guard-boat. After all these preparations the *Chevrette's* men felt both safe and jubilant; but the sight of that French flag flying over the British ensign was a challenge not to be refused, and at half-past nine that night the boats of the three frigates—the *Doris*, the *Uranie*, and the *Beaulieu*—fifteen in all, carrying 280 officers and men, were in the water and pulling off to attack the *Chevrette*.

Lieutenant Losack, in command, with his own and five other boats, suddenly swung off in the gloom in chase of what he supposed to be the look-out boat of the enemy, ordering the other nine boats to lie on their oars till he returned. But time stole on; he failed to return; and Lieutenant Maxwell, the next in command, reflecting that the night was going, and the boats had six miles to pull, determined to carry out the expedition, though he had only nine boats and less than 180 men, instead of fifteen boats and 280 men. He summoned his little squadron in the darkness about him, and gave exact instructions. As the boats dashed up, one was to cut the *Chevrette's* cables; when they boarded, the smartest topmen, named man by man, were to fight their way aloft and cut loose the *Chevrette's* sails; one of the finest sailors in the boats, Wallis, the quartermaster of the Beaulieu, was to take charge of the *Chevrette's* helm. Thus at one and the same instant the *Chevrette* was to be boarded, cut loose, its sails dropped, and its head swung round towards the harbour mouth.

At half-past twelve the moon sank. The night was windless and black; but the bearing of the *Chevrette* had been taken by compass, and the boats pulled gently on, till, ghost-like in the gloom, the doomed ship was discernible. A soft air from the land began to blow at that moment. Suddenly the *Chevrette* and the batteries overhead broke into flame. The boats were discovered! The officers leaped to their feet in the stern of each boat, and urged the men on. The leading boats crashed against the *Chevrette's* side. The ship was boarded simultaneously on both bows and quarters. The force on board the *Chevrette*, however, was numerous enough to make a triple line of armed men round the whole sweep of its bulwarks; they were armed with pikes, tomahawks, cutlasses, and muskets, and they met the attack most gallantly, even venturing in their turn to board the boats. By this time, however, the nine boats Maxwell was leading had all come up, and although the defence outnumbered the attack by more than two to one, yet the British were not to be denied. They clambered fiercely on board; the topmen raced aloft, found the foot-ropes on the yards all strapped up, but running out, cutlass in hand, they cut loose the *Chevrette's* sails. Wallis, meanwhile, had fought his way to the wheel, slew two of the enemy in the process, was desperately wounded himself, yet stood steadily at the wheel, and kept the *Chevrette* under command, the batteries by this time opening upon the ship a fire of grape and heavy shot.

In less than three minutes after the boats came alongside, although nearly every second man of their crews had been killed or wounded, the three topsails and courses of the *Chevrette* had fallen, the cables had been cut, and the ship was moving out in the darkness. She leaned over to the light breeze, the ripple sounded louder at her stern, and when the French felt the ship under movement, it for the moment paralysed their defence. Some jumped overboard; others threw down their arms and ran below. The fight, though short, had been so fierce that the deck was simply strewn with bodies. Many of the French who had retreated below renewed the fight there; they tried to blow up the quarter-deck with gunpowder in their desperation, and the British had to fight a new battle between decks with half their force while the ship was slowly getting under weigh. The fire of the batteries was furious, but, curiously enough, no important spar was struck, though some of the boats towing alongside were sunk. And while the batteries thundered overhead, and the battle still raged on the decks below, the British seamen managed to set every sail on the ship, and even got topgallant yards across. Slowly the *Chevrette* drew out of the harbour. Just then some boats were discovered pulling furiously up through the darkness; they were taken to be French boats bent on recapture, and Maxwell's almost exhausted seamen were summoned to a new conflict. The approaching boats, however, turned out to be the detachment under Lieutenant Losack, who came up to find the work done and the *Chevrette* captured.

The fight on the deck of the *Chevrette* had been of a singularly deadly character. The British had a total of 11 killed and 57 wounded; the *Chevrette* lost 92 killed and 62 wounded, amongst the slain being the *Chevrette's* captain, her two lieutenants, and three midshipmen. Many stories are told of the daring displayed by British seamen in this attack. The boatswain of the *Beaulieu*, for example, boarded the *Chevrette's* taffrail; he took one glance along the crowded decks, waved his cutlass, shouted "Make a lane there!" and literally carved his way through to the forecastle, which he cleared of the French, and kept clear, in spite of repeated attacks, while he assisted to cast the ship about and make sail with as much coolness as though he had been on board the *Beaulieu*. Wallis, who fought his way to the helm of the *Chevrette*, and, though wounded, kept his post with iron coolness while the fight raged, was accosted by his officer when the fight was over with an expression of sympathy for his wounds. "It is only a prick or two, sir," said Wallis, and he added he "was ready to go out on a similar expedition the next night." A boatswain's mate named Ware had his left arm cut clean off by a furious slash of a French sabre, and fell back into the boat. With the help of a comrade's tarry fingers Ware bound up the bleeding stump with rough but energetic surgery, climbed with his solitary hand on board the *Chevrette*, and played a most gallant part in the fight.

The fight that captured the *Chevrette* is almost without parallel. Here was a ship carried off from an enemy's port, with the combined fleets of France and Spain looking on. The enemy were not taken by surprise; they did not merely defy attack, they invited it. The British had to assail a force three times their number, with every advantage of situation and arms. The British boats were exposed to a heavy fire from the *Chevrette* itself and from the shore batteries before they came alongside. The crews fought their way up the sides of the ship in the face of overwhelming odds; they got the vessel under weigh while the fight still raged, and brought her out of a narrow and difficult roadstead, before they had actually captured her. "All this was done," to quote the *Naval Chronicle* for 1802, "in the presence of the grand fleet of the enemy; it was done by nine boats out of fifteen, which originally set out upon the expedition; it was done under the conduct of an officer who, in the absence of the person appointed to command, undertook it upon his own responsibility, and whose intrepidity, judgment, and presence of mind, seconded by the wonderful exertions of the officers and men under his command, succeeded in effecting an enterprise which, by those who reflect upon its peculiar circumstances, will ever be regarded with astonishment."

ALSO FROM LEONAUR
AVAILABLE IN SOFTCOVER OR HARDCOVER WITH DUST JACKET

SEPOYS, SIEGE & STORM *by Charles John Griffiths*—The Experiences of a young officer of H.M.'s 61st Regiment at Ferozepore, Delhi ridge and at the fall of Delhi during the Indian mutiny 1857.

CAMPAIGNING IN ZULULAND *by W. E. Montague*—Experiences on campaign during the Zulu war of 1879 with the 94th Regiment.

THE STORY OF THE GUIDES *by G. J. Younghusband*—The Exploits of the Soldiers of the famous Indian Army Regiment from the northwest frontier 1847 - 1900..

ZULU: 1879 *by D.C.F. Moodie & the Leonaur Editors*—The Anglo-Zulu War of 1879 from contemporary sources: First Hand Accounts, Interviews, Dispatches, Official Documents & Newspaper Reports.

THE RECOLLECTIONS OF SKINNER OF SKINNER'S HORSE *by James Skinner*—James Skinner and his 'Yellow Boys' Irregular cavalry in the wars of India between the British, Mahratta, Rajput, Mogul, Sikh & Pindarree Forces.

TOMMY ATKINS' WAR STORIES 14 FIRST HAND ACCOUNTS—Fourteen first hand accounts from the ranks of the British Army during Queen Victoria's Empire Original & True Battle Stories Recollections of the Indian Mutiny With the 49th in the Crimea With the Guards in Egypt The Charge of the Six Hundred With Wolseley in Ashanti Alma, Inkermann and Magdala With the Gunners at Tel-el-Kebir Russian Guns and Indian Rebels Rough Work in the Crimea In the Maori Rising Facing the Zulus From Sebastopol to Lucknow Sent to Save Gordon On the March to Chitral Tommy by Rudyard Kipling

CHASSEUR OF 1914 *by Marcel Dupont*—Experiences of the twilight of the French Light Cavalry by a young officer during the early battles of the great war in Europe.

TROOP HORSE & TRENCH *by R. A. Lloyd*—The experiences of a British Lifeguardsman of the household cavalry fighting on the western front during the First World War 1914-18.

THE EAST AFRICAN MOUNTED RIFLES *by C. J. Wilson*—Experiences of the campaign in the East African bush during the First World War.

THE FIGHTING CAMELIERS *by Frank Reid*—The exploits of the Imperial Camel Corps in the desert and Palestine campaigns of the First World War.

LEONAUR

ALSO FROM LEONAUR
AVAILABLE IN SOFTCOVER OR HARDCOVER WITH DUST JACKET

THE COMPLEAT RIFLEMAN HARRIS *by Benjamin Harris as told to & transcribed by Captain Henry Curling*—The adventures of a soldier of the 95th (Rifles) during the Peninsular Campaign of the Napoleonic Wars

WITH WELLINGTON'S LIGHT CAVALRY *by William Tomkinson*—The Experiences of an officer of the 16th Light Dragoons in the Peninsular and Waterloo campaigns of the Napoleonic Wars.

SERGEANT BOURGOGNE *by Adrien Bourgogne*—With Napoleon's Imperial Guard in the Russian Campaign and on the Retreat from Moscow 1812 - 13.

SWORDS OF HONOUR *by Henry Newbolt & Stanley L. Wood*—The Careers of Six Outstanding Officers from the Napoleonic Wars, the Wars for India and the American Civil War, with dozens of illustrations by Stanley L. Wood.

SURTEES OF THE RIFLES *by William Surtees*—A Soldier of the 95th (Rifles) in the Peninsular campaign of the Napoleonic Wars.

ENSIGN BELL IN THE PENINSULAR WAR *by George Bell*—The Experiences of a young British Soldier of the 34th Regiment 'The Cumberland Gentlemen' in the Napoleonic wars.

HUSSAR IN WINTER *by Alexander Gordon*—A British Cavalry Officer during the retreat to Corunna in the Peninsular campaign of the Napoleonic Wars.

NAPOLEONIC WAR STORIES *by Sir Arthur Quiller-Couch*—Tales of soldiers, spies, battles & sieges from the Peninsular & Waterloo campaingns.

JOURNALS OF ROBERT ROGERS OF THE RANGERS *by Robert Rogers*—The exploits of Rogers & the Rangers in his own words during 1755-1761 in the French & Indian War.

KERSHAW'S BRIGADE VOLUME 1 *by D. Augustus Dickert*—Manassas, Seven Pines, Sharpsburg (Antietam), Fredricksburg, Chancellorsville, Gettysburg, Chickamauga, Chattanooga, Fort Sanders & Bean Station..

KERSHAW'S BRIGADE VOLUME 2 *by D. Augustus Dickert*—At the wilderness, Cold Harbour, Petersburg, The Shenandoah Valley and Cedar Creek.

A TIGER ON HORSEBACK *by L. March Phillips*—The Experiences of a Trooper & Officer of Rimington's Guides - The Tigers - during the Anglo-Boer war 1899 - 1902.

Printed in the United States
94387LV00005B/6/A